First World War
and Army of Occupation
War Diary
France, Belgium and Germany

3 CAVALRY DIVISION
Divisional Troops
Royal Army Medical Corps
8 Cavalry Field Ambulance
4 December 1914 - 11 April 1918

WO95/1148/2

The Naval & Military Press Ltd
www.nmarchive.com
Published in association with The National Archives

Published by

The Naval & Military Press Ltd

Unit 10 Ridgewood Industrial Park,

Uckfield, East Sussex,

TN22 5QE England

Tel: +44 (0) 1825 749494

www.naval-military-press.com

www.nmarchive.com

This diary has been reprinted in facsimile from the original. Any imperfections are inevitably reproduced and the quality may fall short of modern type and cartographic standards.

© **Crown Copyright**
Images reproduced by permission of The National Archives, London, England, 2015.

Contents

Document type	Place/Title	Date From	Date To
Heading	1914-1918 3rd Cavalry Division No. 8 Cavalry Field Ambulance Dec 1914-Apl 1918		
Heading	8th Cavalry Field Ambulance Vol I Dec 1914-Apl 1918		
War Diary	Driffield	04/12/1914	04/12/1914
War Diary	Southampton	05/12/1914	15/12/1914
War Diary	Havre	16/12/1914	18/12/1914
War Diary	Hazebrouck	23/12/1914	29/12/1914
War Diary	Havre	19/12/1914	20/12/1914
War Diary	Neuf Chatel	21/12/1914	21/12/1914
War Diary	Hazebrouck	22/12/1914	31/12/1914
Heading	No 8 Cavalry Field Ambulance Vol II		
War Diary	Hazebrouck	01/01/1915	27/01/1915
War Diary	Ebblinghem	29/01/1915	31/01/1915
Heading	8th Cavalry Field Ambulance Vol III		
War Diary	Ebblinghem	01/02/1915	03/02/1915
War Diary	Ypres	03/02/1915	14/02/1915
War Diary	Ebblinghem	14/02/1915	28/02/1915
Heading	8th Cavalry Field Ambulance Vol IV		
War Diary	Ebblinghem	01/03/1915	09/03/1915
War Diary	Blaringhem Sec Bois	11/03/1915	13/03/1915
War Diary	Blaringhem	13/03/1915	31/03/1915
Heading	No 8 Cavalry Field Ambulance Vol V		
War Diary	Blaringhem	01/04/1915	05/04/1915
War Diary	Ebblinghem	06/04/1915	11/04/1915
War Diary	La Moulin Fontaine	12/04/1915	13/04/1915
War Diary	Blaringhem	14/04/1915	22/04/1915
War Diary	La'beele	23/04/1915	23/04/1915
War Diary	Vlamertinghe	24/04/1915	24/04/1915
War Diary	Oudezeele	25/04/1915	25/04/1915
War Diary	I Mile S.W. Of Poperinghe on Poperinghe L'Abeele Rd	26/04/1915	27/04/1915
War Diary	Farm 1 Mile N E Of Steenvoor de Near Hill 20 (Ref Map Hazebrouck R (a)	28/04/1915	29/04/1915
War Diary	Farm 1 Mile N.E. Of Steenvoor de Near Hell 20.	30/04/1915	30/04/1915
Heading	3rd Cavalry Division No. 8 Cavalry Field Ambulance Vol VI		
War Diary	Farm one Mile N.E. of Steenvoorde Near Hill 20	01/05/1915	03/05/1915
War Diary	Point 35 Ref Map Hazebrouck & Houtkerque	04/05/1915	04/05/1915
War Diary	Houtkerque	05/05/1915	06/05/1915
War Diary	Blaringhem	07/05/1915	08/05/1915
War Diary	Pt 35 (Ref Map Hazebrouck Va)	09/05/1915	20/05/1915
War Diary	Blaringhem	21/05/1915	28/05/1915
War Diary	Vlamertinghe	29/05/1915	31/05/1915
Heading	3rd Cavalry Division No. 8 Cavalry Field Ambulance Vol VII		
War Diary	Vlamertinghe	01/06/1915	06/06/1915
War Diary	Blaringhem	07/06/1915	30/06/1915
Heading	8th Cavalry Field Ambulance Vol VIII From 1st to 31st July 1915		
War Diary	Blaringhem	01/07/1915	31/07/1915

Heading	3rd Cavalry Division No. 8 Cary Field Ambulance Vol IX August 15		
War Diary	Blaringhem	01/08/1915	06/08/1915
War Diary	Petigny	06/08/1915	09/08/1915
War Diary	Petigny & Bomy	10/08/1915	10/08/1915
War Diary	Bomy	11/08/1915	31/08/1915
Heading	3rd Cavalry Division 8th Cary. Field Ambulance Vol X Sept 15		
War Diary	Bomy	01/09/1915	21/09/1915
War Diary	Labeuvriere	22/09/1915	25/09/1915
War Diary	Novelles-Lez-Vermelles	26/09/1915	27/09/1915
War Diary	Philosophe	27/09/1915	29/09/1915
War Diary	Labeuvriere	30/09/1915	30/09/1915
Heading	3rd Cavalry Division 8th Cav Fd. Amb Oct 15 Vol XI		
War Diary	Labeuvriere	01/10/1915	03/10/1915
War Diary	Burbure	04/10/1915	19/10/1915
War Diary	Reclinghem	20/10/1915	21/10/1915
War Diary	Beaumetz-Les-Aire	22/10/1915	31/10/1915
Heading	3rd Cavalry Division No. 8 Cav. Fd. Amb. Nov. 1915 Vol XII		
War Diary	Beaumetz-Les-Aire	01/11/1915	02/11/1915
War Diary	St. Leger	02/11/1915	02/11/1915
War Diary	Lynde	03/11/1915	09/11/1915
War Diary	Ouderdom	09/11/1915	09/11/1915
War Diary	Lynde	10/11/1915	10/11/1915
War Diary	Beaumetz-Les-Aire	11/11/1915	17/11/1915
War Diary	Rimboval	18/11/1915	30/11/1915
Heading	8th Cav. Fd. Amb. Dec Vol XIII		
War Diary	Rimboval	01/12/1915	31/12/1915
Heading	8 Cav. Fd. Amb. Vol XIV		
War Diary	Rimboval	01/01/1916	29/02/1916
Heading	8th Cav. Field Ambulance		
Heading	8 Cav Fd Amb Vol XV		
War Diary	Rimboval	01/03/1916	31/03/1916
Heading	War Diary of No. 8 Cav. Field Ambulance For April 1916		
Heading	8 Cav Fd Amb Vol XVI		
War Diary	Rimboval	01/04/1916	30/04/1916
Heading	3rd Cav Div 8th Cav Fd May 1916		
Miscellaneous	D.A.G 3rd Echelon Base	05/06/1916	05/06/1916
War Diary	Rimboval	01/05/1916	14/05/1916
War Diary	Noyelle En Chaussee	15/05/1916	21/05/1916
War Diary	Rimboval	22/05/1916	31/05/1916
Heading	3rd Cav Div 8th Cavalry Field Ambulance June 1916		
War Diary	Merlimont	01/06/1916	10/06/1916
War Diary	Rimboval	11/06/1916	24/06/1916
War Diary	Regniere-Ecluse	25/06/1916	25/06/1916
War Diary	Stouen	26/06/1916	26/06/1916
War Diary	Bonnay	27/06/1916	30/06/1916
Heading	War Diary of 8 Cav Fd Ambulance For July 1916		
War Diary	Bonnay	01/07/1916	04/07/1916
War Diary	Bailleul	05/07/1916	09/07/1916
War Diary	Bonnay	09/07/1916	31/07/1916
Heading	Diary Of 8th Cavalry Field Ambulance Month Of August 1916 Vol 20		
War Diary	Bonnay	01/08/1916	01/08/1916

War Diary	St Pierre A Gouy	02/08/1916	02/08/1916
War Diary	Neuilly L'Hopital	03/08/1916	03/08/1916
War Diary	Douriez	04/08/1916	04/08/1916
War Diary	Blingel	05/08/1916	31/08/1916
Heading	8th Cav Fd Ambulance Sept 1916		
Heading	Diary Of 8th Cavalry Field Ambulance September 1916 Vol 21		
War Diary	Blingel	01/09/1916	10/09/1916
War Diary	Douriez	11/09/1916	11/09/1916
War Diary	St. Riquier	12/09/1916	12/09/1916
War Diary	St Saveur	13/09/1916	14/09/1916
War Diary	X Area N Of Bussy	15/09/1916	15/09/1916
War Diary	Laneuville	16/09/1916	17/09/1916
War Diary	Vecquemont	18/09/1916	22/09/1916
War Diary	L'Etoile	23/09/1916	23/09/1916
War Diary	Rougefay	24/09/1916	24/09/1916
War Diary	Bois Jean	25/09/1916	30/09/1916
Heading	8th Cavalry Field Ambulance Oct 1916		
Heading	War Diary of No. 8 Cavalry Field Ambulance October 1916		
War Diary	Beurain. Ch	01/10/1916	02/10/1916
War Diary	Brimeux	03/10/1916	26/10/1916
War Diary	Hesmond	27/10/1916	31/10/1916
Heading	War Diary of No. 8 Cav Field Ambulance For Month Of November 1916		
War Diary	Hesmond	01/11/1916	30/11/1916
Heading	War Diary of 8th Cav. Field Ambulance December 1916		
War Diary	Hesmond	01/12/1916	22/12/1916
War Diary	Merlimont Plage	23/12/1916	31/12/1916
Heading	Diary Of 8th Cav. Field Ambulance January 1917 Vol 25		
War Diary	Merlimont Plage	01/01/1917	31/01/1917
Heading	War Diary of No. 8 Cavalry Field Ambulance February 1917 Vol 26		
War Diary	Fruges	01/02/1917	28/02/1917
Heading	War Diary of 8th Cavalry Field Ambulance Month Of March 1917		
War Diary	Fruges	01/03/1917	31/03/1917
Heading	War Diary of No. 8 Cavalry Field Ambulance For April 1917 Vol 28		
Heading	Summary Of Medical War Diaries Of 8th Cavalry Field Ambulance		
Miscellaneous	8th Cavalry F.A. 3rd Cav. Div. Cav. Corps		
War Diary	Fruges	01/04/1917	05/04/1917
War Diary	Fressin	06/04/1917	08/04/1917
War Diary	Frevent	08/04/1917	08/04/1917
War Diary	Gony En Artois	09/04/1917	09/04/1917
War Diary	Arras Area	10/04/1917	10/04/1917
War Diary	H 34 Central Ref Map 51 B 1-40000	11/04/1917	11/04/1917
War Diary	Orange Hill Area	12/04/1917	12/04/1917
War Diary	Gouy En Artois	13/04/1917	14/04/1917
War Diary	Gouy	15/04/1917	16/04/1917
War Diary	Gouy En Artois	17/04/1917	17/04/1917
War Diary	Barly	18/04/1917	19/04/1917
War Diary	Chateauy Romont	20/04/1917	23/04/1917

War Diary	Lespinoy	24/04/1917	30/04/1917
Heading	War Diary of No. 8 Cavalry Field Ambulance For The Month Of May 1917 Vol 25		
Heading	Summary Of Medical War Diaries Of 8th Cavalry Field Ambulance		
Miscellaneous	8th Cavalry F.A.		
War Diary	Romont Ch	01/05/1917	12/05/1917
War Diary	Guigny	13/05/1917	13/05/1917
War Diary	Vaulx	14/05/1917	14/05/1917
War Diary	Frohen Le.Grand	15/05/1917	15/05/1917
War Diary	Talmas	16/05/1917	16/05/1917
War Diary	Pont Noyelles	17/05/1917	17/05/1917
War Diary	Hamel	18/05/1917	19/05/1917
War Diary	Buire	20/05/1917	31/05/1917
Heading	No. 8 Cav. F.A June 1917		
Heading	War Diary 8th L.F. Amb Month Of June 1917 Vol 30		
War Diary	Buire	01/06/1917	11/06/1917
War Diary	Epehy	12/06/1917	22/06/1917
War Diary	Buire	23/06/1917	30/06/1917
Heading	War Diary of 8th C.F. Ambulance For Month Of July 1917 Vol 31		
War Diary	Buire	01/07/1917	01/07/1917
War Diary	Suzanne	02/07/1917	02/07/1917
War Diary	Treux	03/07/1917	03/07/1917
War Diary	Freschevillers	04/07/1917	04/07/1917
War Diary	Rebreuviette	05/07/1917	05/07/1917
War Diary	Antigneul Chateau	06/07/1917	16/07/1917
War Diary	Thiennes	17/07/1917	31/07/1917
Heading	War Diary of No. 8 Cav. Field Ambulance For The Month Of September 1917 Vol 33		
War Diary	Ham En Artois	01/09/1917	30/09/1917
Heading	War Diary of No. 8 Cavalry Field Ambulance For Month Of August 1917		
War Diary	Thiennes	01/08/1917	09/08/1917
War Diary	Ham-En-Artois	10/08/1917	31/08/1917
Heading	War Diary 8th Cav. Field Ambulance For Month Of October 1917		
War Diary	Ham-En-Artois	01/10/1917	10/10/1917
War Diary	Asile D'Aliennes St Venant	11/10/1917	16/10/1917
War Diary	Bours	17/10/1917	20/10/1917
War Diary	Houvin Houvigneul	21/10/1917	21/10/1917
War Diary	Vignacourt	22/10/1917	31/10/1917
Heading	No. 8. Cav. F.A. Nov 1917		
War Diary	Vignacourt	01/11/1917	18/11/1917
War Diary	Bray	19/11/1917	22/11/1917
War Diary	Poulainville	23/11/1917	30/11/1917
Heading	No. 8. Cav. F.A. Dec 1917		
War Diary	Poulainville	01/12/1917	01/12/1917
War Diary	Belloy of Somme	02/12/1917	31/12/1917
Heading	No. 8 Cav. F.a.		
War Diary	Belloy of Somme	01/01/1918	26/01/1918
War Diary	Guillaucourt	27/01/1918	27/01/1918
War Diary	Tertry	28/01/1918	31/01/1918
Heading	No. 8 Cav. F.a. Feb 1918		
War Diary	Tertry	01/02/1918	28/02/1918
Heading	No. 8 Cav. F.A. Mar 1918		

War Diary	Tertry	01/03/1918	10/03/1918
War Diary	Guignemicourt	11/03/1918	11/03/1918
War Diary	Domart	12/03/1918	12/03/1918
War Diary	Villers Sous Ailly	13/03/1918	31/03/1918
Heading	8th Cavalry Field Amb Apr 1918		
War Diary	Villers Sous Auth	01/04/1918	11/04/1918

1914-1918
3RD CAVALRY DIVISION

NO.8 CAVALRY FIELD AMBULANCE

DEC 1 914 - APL 1918

8th Cavalry Field Ambulance.

Vol I.

Dec 1914 — Apr 1918

Army Form C. 2118.

WAR DIARY
or
INTELLIGENCE SUMMARY

(Erase heading not required.)

Instructions regarding War Diaries and Intelligence Summaries are contained in F. S. Regs, Part II. and the Staff Manual respectively. Title pages will be prepared in manuscript.

Hour, Date, Place	Summary of Events and Information	Remarks and references to Appendices
11-45 p.m. Dec 4th 1914. DRIFFIELD	Entraining for SOUTHAMPTON with the whole of the Unit consisting of 4 Officers, 9 ninety-nine other ranks together forty-six horses, two Maltese Ambulance Wagons two Medical Store Wagons (improvised) two baggage Wagons (improvised) and one field cart.	S.o.S.
10.0 am Dec 5th 1914. SOUTHAMPTON	Arrived at SOUTHAMPTON met at the station by the Embarkation Officer who directed us to proceed to the Rest Camp. The Commissariat Motor Ambulance, 1 motor cycle, 1 sergt, 14 drivers A.S.C. Mech. Transport were taken on the strength. Reported arrival to the Camp adjutant.	S.o.S.
Dec 6th 1914. SOUTHAMPTON.	The Unit was inspected by CAPT. HUTCHINSON on behalf of GENERAL BETHUNE. Also inspected by A.S.C. Officer from ALDERSHOT.	S.o.S.
7th Dec 1914. SOUTHAMPTON.	The following A.S.C. details reported themselves were taken on strength. 1 Saddler, 1 Wheeler, 2 Shoeing Smiths & 8 drivers.	S.o.S.
8th Dec 1914 SOUTHAMPTON.	No 1147. Pvt SENIOR was sent to Military Hospital NETLEY suffering from appendicitis.	S.o.S.
9th Dec 1914. SOUTHAMPTON.	No 144 Pte BIRKINSHAW from the Reserve Unit-reported himself to replace Pvt SENIOR was taken on to strength. The Unit was inspected by MAJOR. McSHEEN from the War Office.	S.o.S.

WAR DIARY
or
INTELLIGENCE SUMMARY

(Erase heading not required.)

Army Form C. 2118.

Hour, Date, Place	Summary of Events and Information	Remarks and references to Appendices
10th Dec 1914 SOUTHAMPTON	Waiting for receiving new equipment, the unit is in accordance with "Provincial Establishments". Wanted Maypole Field Ambulances dated Dec 3, 1914.	
11th Dec "	Telephone messages with reference to new equipment sent	
12th Dec "	daily to War Office.	
13th Dec "		S.O.S.
14th Dec 1914 SOUTHAMPTON	Enrolled of Driver CARL AUGUST DELLSCHAFT, of A.S.C. M.T. attached to the unit was examined. Purposely Quarter reported to Camp Adjutant. Telegram sent to SCOTLAND YARD asking the police to make enquiries as to the antecedents of Dvr DELLSCHAFT. Reply received late in the evening stating that enquiries had been made & that its police knew nothing of him, but that further enquiries would be made. Received instructions to be prepared to embark on the AFRICAN PRINCE at 10.30 am on the following day.	S.P.R.

WAR DIARY
or
INTELLIGENCE SUMMARY
(Erase heading not required.)

Army Form C. 2118.

Hour, Date, Place	Summary of Events and Information	Remarks and references to Appendices
9. a.m. 15th Dec 1914. SOUTHAMPTON.	Saw the PROVOST. MARSHALL. CAPT. RATIGAN. with reference to CARL AUGUST. DELL SCHAFT. Enforced reply received from SCOTLAND.YARD. concerning of Left. CPL. AUGUST DELL SCHAFT in charge of the Camp. Commandant together with written report giving reasons for leaving him behind.	S/S
11. a.m. Dec 15th 1914. SOUTHAMPTON.	Embarked on AFRICAN. PRINCE. for FRANCE with complete Unit except 7 Motor Ambulances, 1 Motor Cycle + 1 Sergt - 13 men. of A.S.C. M.T. who embarked on the TINTORETTO.	S/S
9. a.m. 16th Dec 1914. HAVRE.	The Unit disembarked now instructed by the Disembarkation officer to proceed to No.2 REST CAMP. SAN.VIC. Arrival reported to BASE. Commandant.	S/S
17. Dec 1914. HAVRE.	Inspection by Camp Commandant.	S/S
18 Dec 1914. HAVRE.	The Rifles of 16 A.S.C. details were inspect. Sent to the Ordnance Depot. examined. some were found incapable of taking Govt. New Ammunition, were changed. Received new ammunition to proceed by train to ST. OMER. the following day, a French Ellipolis reported himself.	S/S

Army Form C. 2118.

WAR DIARY
or
INTELLIGENCE SUMMARY

(Erase heading not required.)

Instructions regarding War Diaries and Intelligence Summaries are contained in F. S. Regs., Part II. and the Staff Manual respectively. Title pages will be prepared in manuscript.

Hour, Date, Place	Summary of Events and Information	Remarks and references to Appendices
23rd Dec. 1914. HAZEBROUCK	The Ambz. which had been performed by the 2. 1st Field. Amb. was taken over.	S.A.P.
24th Dec. 1914. HAZEBROUCK	Training A.S.C. M.T. were inoculated against Enteric fever.	S.A.P.
25th Dec. 1914. HAZEBROUCK	Daily routine established. Lectures. Corps duties & marches &c.	S.A.P.
26th Dec. 1914. HAZEBROUCK	Returned part of the Equipment to Ordnance Depôt.	S.A.P.
27th Dec. 1914. HAZEBROUCK	Daily Routine &c.	S.A.P.
28th Dec. 1914. HAZEBROUCK	Visited by D.D.M.S. (Col. WESTCOTT)	S.A.P.
29th Dec. 1914. HAZEBROUCK	One Ambulance Wagon MK. I. Two horses + harness received from HQ Cav. Field. Amb.	S.A.P.

Army Form C. 2118.

WAR DIARY
or
INTELLIGENCE SUMMARY
(Erase heading not required.)

Hour, Date, Place	Summary of Events and Information	Remarks and references to Appendices
3.49 p.m. 19th Dec. 1914. HAVRE.	The Unit with the exception of Lt. Col. W. KITSON CLAYTON, Lt. DOWNIE, INTERPRETER, and its Motor Ambulances Wagons & Lorries arrived at No. 1. POINT. HAVRE from ST. OMER.	S.D.2
8 a.m. 20th Dec. 1914. HAVRE.	LT. COL. CLAYTON, LT. J. DOWNIE and the Motor vehicles arrived left HAVRE for NEUF. CHATTEL. The troop train arrived at ST. OMER at 10 a.m. & there received orders to proceed to HAZEBROUCK, arriving there at 11.0 a.m. & received orders to detrain themselves to billets a mile East of the STATION, arriving there during the afternoon, the Motor transport arrived at NEUF. CHATTELL at 4.0 p.m. and were billeted there for the night.	S.D.2
21st Dec 1914. NEUF. CHATEL.	The Motor transport left NEUF. CHATEL. STOMER about 3.0 p.m. and were billeted between STOMER & HAZEBROUCK via ABBEVILLE joining the rear of its Unit the same evening.	S.D.2
22nd Dec 1914. HAZEBROUCK.	Visited by A.D.M.S. III Cavalry Division accompanied by the D.A.D.M.S. were informed that the Unit would be divided into two Echelons. "A" "B".	S.D.2

Army Form C. 2118.

WAR DIARY
or
~~INTELLIGENCE SUMMARY~~
(Erase heading not required.)

Instructions regarding War Diaries and Intelligence Summaries are contained in F. S. Regs., Part II. and the Staff Manual respectively. Title pages will be prepared in manuscript.

Hour, Date, Place	Summary of Events and Information	Remarks and references to Appendices
30th Dec 1914 HAZEBROUCK	Daily Routine.	S.D.S.
31st Dec 1914 HAZEBROUCK	Two Ambulance Wagons MK. I. received from the 6th Cav: Field. Amb L.".	S.D.S.

Ed. S. Canaby Field Ambulance.

Vol III.

1214327/15
Jan 19 15

Army Form C. 2118.

WAR DIARY
or
INTELLIGENCE SUMMARY
(Erase heading not required.)

Instructions regarding War Diaries and Intelligence Summaries are contained in F. S. Regs., Part II. and the Staff Manual respectively. Title pages will be prepared in manuscript.

Hour, Date, Place	Summary of Events and Information	Remarks and references to Appendices
January 1st 1915 Hazebrook	"B" Echelon, consisting of WO Officers and 64 Other ranks, 4 motor ambulances, 3 horse ambulances, 4 General service waggons, 1 water cart and 1 bicycle, were ordered to proceed to find billets in Hazebrook and receive Supernumeraries taken off the strength of the unit	2D
2nd January 1915 to 3rd January 1915 Hazebrook	Daily Routine	2D
4th January 1915 Hazebrook	No 541 Dvr G. Flack A.S.C. mechanical transport having reported himself to replace a casualty was taken on strength. Notice was received that the III Cavalry Division will be on duty from 8 AM 7th Jan to 8 A.M. 9th Jan 1915.	2D
5th Jan. 1915 to 6th Jan. 1915 Hazebrook		

Army Form C. 2118.

WAR DIARY
or
INTELLIGENCE SUMMARY

(Erase heading not required.)

Instructions regarding War Diaries and Intelligence Summaries are contained in F. S. Regs., Part II. and the Staff Manual respectively. Title pages will be prepared in manuscript.

Hour, Date, Place	Summary of Events and Information	Remarks and references to Appendices
10th January 1915. Hazebrook	"A" Echelon received orders to proceed to billets at No 41 Rue Du Ravage Hazebrook	The billets were found in a very insanitary condition
11th Jan 1915. Hazebrook	The unit was inspected by the D.D.M.S. Colonel O'Keefe	
12 January 1915. Hazebrook	Daily Routine	
13th January 1915. Hazebrook	The unit received notice that the 7th Cavalry Division is on duty from 8 AM 13th Jan. to 8 AM 15th Jan 1915. All ranks in charge of horses one horse dismounted — Strength 30 2D	
14 January 1915. Hazebrook	General Routine	

1247 W 3299 200,000 (E) 8/14 J.B.C. & A. Forms/C. 2118/11.

Army Form C. 2118.

WAR DIARY
or
INTELLIGENCE SUMMARY
(Erase heading not required.)

Instructions regarding War Diaries and Intelligence Summaries are contained in F. S. Regs., Part II. and the Staff Manual respectively. Title pages will be prepared in manuscript.

Hour, Date, Place	Summary of Events and Information	Remarks and references to Appendices
15 January 1915 Hazebrook	Daily Routine	2D
16 January 1915 Hazebrook	Daily Routine	2D
17th January 1915 Hazebrook	Daily Routine	2D Yr. Sullivan went on a weeks leave in another
18st January 1915 Hazebrook	Daily Routine. Lt. E.D. Ellis proceeded on leave to ENGLAND	2D
19 January 1915 Hazebrook	Daily Routine	2D
20 January 1915 Hazebrook	Daily Routine two horse-light draught adds to strength	2D
21 January 1915 Hazebrook	Daily Routine	2D

Army Form C. 2118.

WAR DIARY
or
INTELLIGENCE SUMMARY.
(Erase heading not required.)

Instructions regarding War Diaries and Intelligence Summaries are contained in F. S. Regs., Part II. and the Staff Manual respectively. Title pages will be prepared in manuscript.

Hour, Date, Place	Summary of Events and Information	Remarks and references to Appendices
January 22nd 1915 Hazebrook	Daily Routine	2D
January 23rd 1915 Hazebrook	Daily Routine	
January 24th 1915 Hazebrook	Motor Ambulance, 1 Corporal and 1 man Reconnoitred Brigade on field manoeuvres. Two Limber Waggons, 1 G.S. waggon, fuel tank 8 horses with harness & 4 men A.S.C. drivers joined the unit.	2D 2D 2D
Jan 25th 1915 Hazebrook	Two G.S. waggons with horses & harness complete, also 4 A.S.C drivers handed from A to B Echelon	2D
Jan 26th 1915 Hazebrook	Four horses & two men transferred from D to A Echelon. Received orders to find new billets for unit at EBBINGHAM	2D

(9 29 6) W 4141—463 100,000 9/14 H W V Forms/C. 2118/10

Army Form C. 2118.

WAR DIARY
or
INTELLIGENCE SUMMARY.
(Erase heading not required.)

Hour, Date, Place	Summary of Events and Information	Remarks and references to Appendices
January 24th 1915. HAZEBROOK	A Echelon was inspected by FIELD MARSHALL SIR JOHN FRENCH. Four horses & 2 men transferred from A & B Echelon. Instrns. received from A.D.M.S. III C.D. the unit was ready to move by at 7AM	
January 28th 1915. HAZEBROOK EBBLINGHEM	A Echelon left billets at HAZEBROOK at 1PM, arriving at EBBLINGHEM at 3PM. Billets at FLOUR MILL and houses in the village. Lieut E.D.ELLIS returned from leave.	
January 29th 1915. EBBLINGHEM	Three men of the Mechanical Transport invalided, also 1 Officer head quarters staff. 6 A.S.C. men and 6 men departing	

Army Form C. 2118.

WAR DIARY
or
INTELLIGENCE SUMMARY.

(Erase heading not required.)

Instructions regarding War Diaries and Intelligence Summaries are contained in F. S. Regs., Part II. and the Staff Manual respectively. Title pages will be prepared in manuscript.

Hour, Date, Place	Summary of Events and Information	Remarks and references to Appendices
January 30th 1915. EBBLINGHEM	Officers R.S.C. marched in. Two men A.S.C. attached.	
January 31st 1915. EBBLINGHEM	Two men R.S.C. invalided	

(9 29 6) W 4141—463 100,000 9/14 H W V Forms/C. 2118/10

121/4636

8th Cavalry Field Ambulance

Vol III

Army Form C. 2118.

WAR DIARY
or
INTELLIGENCE SUMMARY.
(Erase heading not required.)

Instructions regarding War Diaries and Intelligence Summaries are contained in F.S. Regs., Part II. and the Staff Manual respectively. Title pages will be prepared in manuscript.

Hour, Date, Place	Summary of Events and Information	Remarks and references to Appendices
1st Feb 1915. EBBLINGHEM.	General routine.	E.O.E.
2nd Feb 1915. EBBLINGHEM.	General routine	E.O.E.
3rd Feb 1915. EBBLINGHEM.	A part of the Unit proceeded to YPRES to do duty in the trenches. Consisting of Lt. Colonel W. KITSON CLAYTON, MAJOR HAMMERTON 2 M.C. O'St 24 men, 1 motor ambulance, 2 light ambulance wagons (MK I.), 1 Kitchen. G.S. wagon. The water cart belonging to the Unit was sent to Headquarters 8th Cav: Bgde. in charge of 1 driver + 2 worker duty men.	E.O.E.

Army Form C. 2118.

WAR DIARY
or
INTELLIGENCE SUMMARY
(Erase heading not required.)

Instructions regarding War Diaries and Intelligence Summaries are contained in F. S. Regs., Part II. and the Staff Manual respectively. Title pages will be prepared in manuscript.

Hour, Date, Place	Summary of Events and Information	Remarks and references to Appendices
3rd Feb 1915 YPRES.	The detachment for duty in the trenches arrived at YPRES in the afternoon. GJWH	
4th Feb 1915 YPRES.	On duty from 5 p.m. to 5 h.m. next day. At 6 p.m. one officer + 6 men, 2 light amb. wagons were ordered to proceed to the trenches to collect wounded, brought in 10 wounded. GJWH	
5th Feb 1915 YPRES.	On duty until 5 h.m. GJWH	

WAR DIARY
or
INTELLIGENCE SUMMARY

(Erase heading not required.)

Army Form C. 2118.

Hour, Date, Place	Summary of Events and Information	Remarks and references to Appendices
6th Feb 1915. YPRES.	Supplied one medical Officer for duty at Headquarters. G.O.D	
7th Feb 1915. YPRES.	One Medicine Officer, 6 men & 2 light ambulance wagons, collected eleven wounded men, including SURG.- MAJOR COWIE. of the 1st LIFE GUARDS. G.O.D	
8th Feb 1915. YPRES.	One medical Officer 2 horsed ambulance wagons, were sent to HOOGE. to collect wounded, & brought in 9 cases from the Brass Yeomanry. Supplied one medical Officer 6 men, 2 light wagons for duty in MENIN road during evening & night. G.O.D	

Army Form C. 2118.

WAR DIARY
or
INTELLIGENCE SUMMARY
(Erase heading not required.)

Hour, Date, Place	Summary of Events and Information	Remarks and references to Appendices
9th Feb 1915. YPRES.	Supplied one Medical Officer for duty at Divisional Headquarters. Sgd. ??	
10th Feb 1915. YPRES.	One Medical Officer and Motor Ambulance Wagon sent to HOOGE. One Medical Officer T.6 Men with 2 wagons sent to LORD CAVAN's Dug-out. Sgd. ??	
11th Feb 1915. YPRES.	Heavy bombardment of YPRES. Two Officers & 4 Stretcher bearers on duty in the town collecting wounded. Sgd. ??	

WAR DIARY or INTELLIGENCE SUMMARY

Army Form C. 2118.

(Erase heading not required.)

Hour, Date, Place	Summary of Events and Information	Remarks and references to Appendices
12th Feb 1915. YPRES.	Relieved the Medical Officer for duty at divisional Headquarters. The horse which had been sick was sent with the Mobile Veterinary Section. [Gordon]	
13th Feb 1915 YPRES.	The Medical Officer, 6 men & 2 light wagons sent to LORD CAVAN's dug-out to collect wounded. The motor ambulances began sent to HOOGE to collect [Gordon] (wounded).	
14th Feb 1915 YPRES.	Left YPRES at 9.30 a.m. [Gordon] EBBINGHEM. Arrived EBBINGHEM. 6. a. m. [Gordon]	

WAR DIARY
or
INTELLIGENCE SUMMARY.
(Erase heading not required.)

Army Form C. 2118.

Hour, Date, Place	Summary of Events and Information	Remarks and references to Appendices
14th Feb 1915. EBRLINGHEM.	The part of the Unit which has been doing duty - at the Train depot returned, arriving 7. a.m. S.A.B	
15th Feb 1915. EBBLINGHEM.	The following arrived from B. Echelon Men taken on to strength, 2 drivers + 4 horses, to complete the personnel of No 2 Subdivision G.S. Wagon. S.A.B.	
16th Feb 1915. EBRLINGHEM.	Lt. J. DOWNIE + No 9730 S.M. AVDIS went on leave to ENGLAND from the 16th — 23rd. S.A.B.	
17th Feb 1915. EBBLINGHEM.	General Routine. S.A.B.	

WAR DIARY
or
INTELLIGENCE SUMMARY.
(Erase heading not required.)

Army Form C. 2118.

Instructions regarding War Diaries and Intelligence Summaries are contained in F.S. Regs., Part II. and the Staff Manual respectively. Title pages will be prepared in manuscript.

Hour, Date, Place	Summary of Events and Information	Remarks and references to Appendices
18th Feb 1915. EBBLINGHEM.	General routine.	S.D.S.
19th Feb 1915.		
20th Feb 1915. EBBLINGHEM.	No 1216 Pte. W. Cruston was admitted to hospital & transferred to N.5. Casualty Clearing Station	S.D.S.
21st Feb 1915. EBBLINGHEM.	General routine	S.D.S.
22nd Feb 1915. ERBLINGHEM.	General routine	S.D.S.

Army Form C. 2118.

WAR DIARY
or
INTELLIGENCE SUMMARY
(Erase heading not required.)

Instructions regarding War Diaries and Intelligence Summaries are contained in F. S. Regs., Part II. and the Staff Manual respectively. Title pages will be prepared in manuscript.

Hour, Date, Place	Summary of Events and Information	Remarks and references to Appendices
23rd Feb 1915. EBBLINGHEM	General Routine. Lt J. DOWNIE & S. M. AUDUS returned from leave.	
24th Feb 1915. EBBLINGHEM.	General routine. One N.C.O. & two men report themselves from B. Echelon for temporary duty with H. Echelon in relief of three men who were reported to O.C. B. Echelon. Major HAMMERTON & Dr. BARLOW proceeded leave to England.	
25th Feb 1915. EBBLINGHEM	No 1175 Cpe T. DAVIS granted leave to ENGLAND on urgent private affairs. Lt. E.D. ELLIS was appointed temporary Medical Officer of the Force temporarily, Lt WHITE the M. O. being on leave. No 1210 Cpe LEA reported himself from B.Echelon to temporary duty with A. Staff.	

Army Form C. 2118.

WAR DIARY
or
INTELLIGENCE SUMMARY

(Erase heading not required.)

Instructions regarding War Diaries and Intelligence Summaries are contained in F. S. Regs., Part II. and the Staff Manual respectively. Title pages will be prepared in manuscript.

Hour, Date, Place	Summary of Events and Information	Remarks and references to Appendices
26th Feb 1915. EBBLINGHEM	General routine. One horse sent to Mobile Veterinary Section for treatment from Battery at full strength.	9.0.8.
27th Feb 1915. EBBLINGHEM	General routine.	9.0.8.
28th Feb 1915. EBBLINGHEM	General routine. Major HAMMERTON returned from leave.	9.0.8.

M.W. White Captain R.F.A.

8th Cavalry Field Ambulance

Vol IV

1 March 1915

Army Form C. 2118.

WAR DIARY
or
INTELLIGENCE SUMMARY

(Erase heading not required.)

Instructions regarding War Diaries and Intelligence Summaries are contained in F. S. Regs., Part II. and the Staff Manual respectively. Title pages will be prepared in manuscript.

Hour, Date, Place	Summary of Events and Information	Remarks and references to Appendices
1st March 1915. EBBLINGHEM	Daily routine. No 1175 Corpl DAVIS T. on special leave to ENGLAND is granted extension up to and including 9th inst. JD	
2nd March 1915. EBBLINGHEM	Daily Routine. No M35-486 Dr COUSINS H. ASC MT reported himself from base transport Depot HAVRE to replace casualty 9 was taken in charge. No 42 Pte BOWLES E. RAMC. has been admitted to hospital and transferred to No 5- C.C.S. 9 taken off strength of unit. One officers charger taken on strength. JD	
3rd March 1915. EBBLINGHEM	MAJOR HAMMERTON transferred from duty to B. echelon also 3 N.C.O's 4 drivers and 2 privates. Two N.C.O.s 4 privates and 3 drivers transferred from B. to A echelon. The above transfers are in accordance with new organization scheme. JD	

Army Form C. 2118.

WAR DIARY
or
INTELLIGENCE SUMMARY

(Erase heading not required.)

Instructions regarding War Diaries and Intelligence Summaries are contained in F. S. Regs, Part II. and the Staff Manual respectively. Title pages will be prepared in manuscript.

Hour, Date, Place	Summary of Events and Information	Remarks and references to Appendices
4th Mar 1915. EBBLINGHEM	Daily Routine. No 1033 L.Cpl CROWTHER C. appointed acting Sergt. on probation dated 3/3/15. 2D	
5th Mar 1915. EBBLINGHEM	Daily Routine. No 1009 Corpl FALLON J. granted leave to proceed to ENGLAND up to and including 8th inst. 2D	
6th Mar 1915. EBBLINGHEM	Daily Routine. 2D	

Army Form C. 2118.

WAR DIARY
or
INTELLIGENCE SUMMARY
(Erase heading not required.)

Instructions regarding War Diaries and Intelligence Summaries are contained in F.S. Regs., Part II. and the Staff Manual respectively. Title pages will be prepared in manuscript.

Hour, Date, Place	Summary of Events and Information	Remarks and references to Appendices
May 7th 1915 EBBLINGHEM May 8th 1915	Daily Routine	
EBBLINGHEM May 9th 1915	Daily Routine 2D No 1176 Corp¹ DAVIS T and 1007 Corp² FALLON I returned from leave. Orders received from Brigade Headquarters for the Bind to be prepared to move off at 6 AM the following morning 2D	
May 10th 1915 EBBLINGHEM BLARINGHEM	Received orders to "stand by" at 2.30 acting according to instructions from Brigade Head Quarters left Billets in EBBLINGHEM and forward to BLARINGHEM. Received orders to move at 5 AM next t morning with the brigade 2D	

WAR DIARY
or
INTELLIGENCE SUMMARY
(Erase heading not required.)

Army Form C. 2118.

Hour, Date, Place	Summary of Events and Information	Remarks and references to Appendices
Mar 11th 1915 BLARINGHEM SEC BOIS	Left BLARINGHEM and following in rear of Battery formerly "A" Echelon arrived at LA MOTT at 4.30 A.M. Stood by until 4 PM when instructions were received to proceed to SEC BOIS and be prepared to move at short notice. At 11 PM orders were received to be prepared to move. Tf at 6 AM the following morning. On this day No 1160 Pte LOCKWOOD was granted 5 days sp[ecia]l leave to ENGLAND	

Army Form C. 2118.

WAR DIARY
or
INTELLIGENCE SUMMARY

(Erase heading not required.)

Instructions regarding War Diaries and Intelligence Summaries are contained in F. S. Regs., Part II. and the Staff Manual respectively. Title pages will be prepared in manuscript.

Hour, Date, Place	Summary of Events and Information	Remarks and references to Appendices
May 12th 1915. SEC. BOIS	Unit was ready to march off at 6 AM and remained standing by all day. Sergt. VIPOND a.s.c. m.m. and the motor cycle went for reserves from B to A Echelon. The following reinforcements were received from reinforcement depot: 1 riding horse, 1 A Echelon 4 light draught horses, 6 Echelon from Beekelar. 11 light draught horses were sent to ADVS (?) 28th divisionary. In the evening instructions were received to be prepared to move off at 6 AM the following morning. 23	

WAR DIARY
or
INTELLIGENCE SUMMARY

(Erase heading not required.)

Army Form C. 2118.

Hour, Date, Place	Summary of Events and Information	Remarks and references to Appendices
Mar 13th 1915 SEC BOIS BLARINGHEM	The unit was ready to move at 6 AM and remained standing by. Orders were received at 4.30 to start for Lillers at BLARINGHEM at 6.30, via HAZEBROUCK. Arrived at BLARINGHEM at 11 P.M.	
Mar 14th 1915 BLARINGHEM	Still standing by	
Mar 15th 1915 BLARINGHEM	Received orders at 8.10 AM to march off at 6 AM. At 12 noon received orders to be ready at 20 minutes notice. 9 at 3 pm this order was cancelled to 1 hr. 9.20 pm horse light draught horses taken for Strength of B Echelon from the unit abba	

WAR DIARY
or
INTELLIGENCE SUMMARY
(Erase heading not required.)

Army Form C. 2118.

Instructions regarding War Diaries and Intelligence Summaries are contained in F. S. Regs., Part II. and the Staff Manual respectively. Title pages will be prepared in manuscript.

Hour, Date, Place	Summary of Events and Information	Remarks and references to Appendices
Mar 16th 1915 BLARINGHEM	Notice for rendezvous explained to 3 horses & 10 min. Sent 2 light-draught horses to mobile veterinary section 7/0200712 PTE BARLOW A.S.C. returned to from leave. General Routine	
Mar 14th 1915 BLARINGHEM	General Routine No 1160 PTE LOCKWOOD F returned from leave	
Mar 15th 1915 BLARINGHEM	Two light draught horses exchanged at B Echelon by seven of veterinary surgeon	
Mar 19th 1915 BLARINGHEM	General Routine	

Army Form C. 2118.

WAR DIARY
or
INTELLIGENCE SUMMARY.
(Erase heading not required.)

Instructions regarding War Diaries and Intelligence Summaries are contained in F.S. Regs., Part II. and the Staff Manual respectively. Title pages will be prepared in manuscript.

Hour, Date, Place	Summary of Events and Information	Remarks and references to Appendices
Mar 20th 1915 BLARINGHEM	Two Officers 7 men & 14 horses moved to find billets within billeting area	
Mar 21st 1915 BLARINGHEM	General Routine 2D	
Mar 22nd 1915 BLARINGHEM	General Routine 2D	
Mar 23rd 1915 BLARINGHEM	No 1216 Pte CAUSTON W returns from Hospital – Base 2D	

Army Form C. 2118.

WAR DIARY
or
INTELLIGENCE SUMMARY.
(Erase heading not required.)

Instructions regarding War Diaries and Intelligence
Summaries are contained in F. S. Regs., Part II.
and the Staff Manual respectively. Title pages
will be prepared in manuscript.

Hour, Date, Place	Summary of Events and Information	Remarks and references to Appendices
Mar 24th 1915. BLARINGHEM	General Routine	
Mar 25th 1915. BLARINGHEM	R.A.M.C. CAPT HOBBS A/ made a visit from 3rd Erving Hospital. LT GREENWOOD proceeded on 2d Leave to ENGLAND	
Mar 26th 1915. BLARINGHEM	On Office and 19 men of the mobile veterinary section were inoculated against typhus. Inspection of transport by O.C. A.S.C. 3rd Cavalry Division MAJOR GROUSE No 1163 D.r PARKINSON left on special leave to ENGLAND	2D

Army Form C. 2118.

WAR DIARY
or
INTELLIGENCE SUMMARY.

(Erase heading not required.)

Instructions regarding War Diaries and Intelligence Summaries are contained in F.S. Regs., Part II. and the Staff Manual respectively. Title pages will be prepared in manuscript.

Hour, Date, Place	Summary of Events and Information	Remarks and references to Appendices
Mar 27th 1915 BLARINGHEM	Veterinary Officer i/c 20th Mobile Veterinary Section Lt DAVIS inspected the horses of the unit	
Mar 28th 1915 BLARINGHEM	A/S.M Staff STEVENS A.S.C. reported himself from "B" Echelon for one week's duty. 740 A.S- Pte MEREDITH A. removed to No.10 Stationary Hospital suffering from scarlet fever. All necessary precautions re kit &c.9 contacts (running sick) &c. A.D.V.S. 3rd Cavalry Division inspected horses of unit. JD

Army Form C. 2118.

WAR DIARY
or
INTELLIGENCE SUMMARY.
(Erase heading not required.)

Hour, Date, Place	Summary of Events and Information	Remarks and references to Appendices
Mar 29th 1915. BLARINGHEM	The enddr. 9 wheelers from B Echelon returned themselves for 4 days duty	
Mar 30th 1915. BLARINGHEM	General Routine	2D
Mar 31st 1915. BLARINGHEM	General Routine with addition of route march	2D

William Taylor Lt Col

12/5256.

12/5256
April 1915

No 8. Cavalry Field Ambulance

Vol V

Army Form C. 2118.

WAR DIARY
or
INTELLIGENCE SUMMARY.
(Erase heading not required.)

Instructions regarding War Diaries and Intelligence Summaries are contained in F.S. Regs., Part II. and the Staff Manual respectively. Title pages will be prepared in manuscript.

Hour, Date, Place	Summary of Events and Information	Remarks and references to Appendices
April 1st 1915. BLARINGHEM.	General Routine	S.D.2.
April 2nd 1915. BLARINGHEM.	LCOL. W.K. CLAYTON ColGranted 21 days leave. CAPT. J. HOBBS. proceeded to B. ECHELON. Orderly MAJOR HAMMERTON who reported himself at M. Echelon Will assume the position of C.O. during the absence of Lt. Col. CLAYTON. LT. GREENWOOD returned from leave to ENGLAND.	S.D.2.

Army Form C. 2118.

WAR DIARY
or
INTELLIGENCE SUMMARY.
(Erase heading not required.)

Instructions regarding War Diaries and Intelligence Summaries are contained in F. S. Regs., Part II. and the Staff Manual respectively. Title pages will be prepared in manuscript.

Hour, Date, Place	Summary of Events and Information	Remarks and references to Appendices
April 3rd, 1915. BLARINGHEM.	S.M. STEVENS. A.S.C. returned to unit on completion of his duties	See 3
April 4th, 1915. BLARINGHEM.	General Routine.	See 2
April 5th, 1915. BLARINGHEM.	S.M. STEVENS, A.S.C. reports himself for further duty & returns to the unit on the 7th inst.	
April 6th, 1915. EBBLINGHEM.	The Unit having received orders proceeded to be billeted at EBBLINGHEM.	See 3

Army Form C. 2118.

WAR DIARY
or
INTELLIGENCE SUMMARY.
(Erase heading not required.)

Hour, Date, Place	Summary of Events and Information	Remarks and references to Appendices
April 7th 1915. EBBLINGHEM.	The Unit was inspected by the ADMS 3rd Cavalry Division Col. BEWLAY. S.M. STEVENS Returned to the Unit.	S.D.?
April 8th 1915. EBBLINGHEM.	S. Sgt White granted special leave to ENGLAND from 8th — 15th April.	S.D.?
April 9th 1915. EBBLINGHEM.	The Unit was the Brigadier at 11 a.m at La PIERRE.	S.D.?
April 10th 1915. EBBLINGHEM.	General Routine.	S.D.?

Army Form C. 2118.

WAR DIARY
or
INTELLIGENCE SUMMARY.
(Erase heading not required.)

Instructions regarding War Diaries and Intelligence Summaries are contained in F. S. Regs., Part II. and the Staff Manual respectively. Title pages will be prepared in manuscript.

Hour, Date, Place	Summary of Events and Information	Remarks and references to Appendices
April 11th 1915. EBBLINGHEM	General Routine	
April 12th 1915. La Moulin Fontaine.	Orders here received to proceed to fulfil at La Moulin Fontaine. One light draught received to replace casualty. D.a.2	
April 13th 1915. La Moulin Fontaine.	General Routine.	
April 14th 1915. BLARINGHEM.	The Unit received orders to proceed to fulfil at BLARINGHEM. (occupied) the position. Lt. GREENWOOD received orders (Farrier) to G. H. Q. Troops Train, having been transferred to that A.S.C.	

WAR DIARY
or
INTELLIGENCE SUMMARY.

(Erase heading not required.)

Army Form C. 2118.

Instructions regarding War Diaries and Intelligence Summaries are contained in F.S. Regs., Part II. and the Staff Manual respectively. Title pages will be prepared in manuscript.

Hour, Date, Place	Summary of Events and Information	Remarks and references to Appendices
April 15th 1915 BLARINGHEM.	Three R.A.M.C.(T.F.) re-inforcement received. To complete establishment four men have attended 1st Class Orderlies. Sgt.	
April 16th 1915 BLARINGHEM.	General Routine. Sgt.	
April 17th 1915 BLARINGHEM.	General Routine. Sgt.	
April 18th 1915 BLARINGHEM.	General Routine. Sgt.	

Army Form C. 2118.

WAR DIARY
or
INTELLIGENCE SUMMARY.
(Erase heading not required.)

Instructions regarding War Diaries and Intelligence Summaries are contained in F. S. Regs., Part II. and the Staff Manual respectively. Title pages will be prepared in manuscript.

Hour, Date, Place	Summary of Events and Information	Remarks and references to Appendices
April 18th 1915 BLARINGHEM	General Routine	E.D.S.
April 19th 1915 BLARINGHEM	General Routine	E.D.S.
April 20th 1915 BLARINGHEM	Motor cars sent to S.C.C. workshops STEENBECQUE for repairs	E.D.S.
April 21st 1915 BLARINGHEM	Four drivers + two Lorries this A.S.C. "A" were transferred from "B" Echelon to the bodies cost with "B" Echelon was lent to the Erase Testmong, during the repairs of their own.	E.D.S.

Army Form C. 2118.

WAR DIARY
or
INTELLIGENCE SUMMARY.
(Erase heading not required.)

Instructions regarding War Diaries and Intelligence Summaries are contained in F.S. Regs, Part II. and the Staff Manual respectively. Title pages will be prepared in manuscript.

Hour, Date, Place	Summary of Events and Information	Remarks and references to Appendices
April 22nd 1915. BLARINGHEM.	The Batt. had a route march with all equipment.	S.O.8
April 23rd 1915. L'ABEELE.	Orders were received at 10 a.m. to proceed as soon as possible to Brigade Rendezvous at SERCUS. The Batt. then proceeded with the Brigade to L'ABEELE billeting for the night 1/2 mile S.E. of the village. (Ref. map HAZEBROUCK Va.).	S.O.8
April 24th 1915. VLAMERTINGHE.	Orders were received to proceed to Cross Roads 1 mile S.W. VLAMERTINGHE. Two Battn. C. reinforcements received. The Batt. billeted for the night at a farm 1 1/2 N. of Nr 35. (Ref. Map HAZEBROUCK Va.)	S.O.4

WAR DIARY
or
INTELLIGENCE SUMMARY

(Erase heading not required.)

Army Form C. 2118.

Hour, Date, Place	Summary of Events and Information	Remarks and references to Appendices
April 25th 1915. OUDEZEELE.	At 9.30 a.m. Unit left billets and proceeded to point 35 S.E. of POPERINGHE. Followed by. Orders were then received (Verbal) to a point 1 mile N.W. of POPERINGHE on the POPERINGHE — CROMBEKE road (Ref mark HAZEBROUCK ½ a). At 3 p.m. Unit proceeded 6 Killers at four cross roads 1 mile S.E. of OUDEZEELE. Sgt 8.	
April 26th 1915. 1 mile S.W. of POPERINGHE on POPERINGHE — L'ABEELE Rd.	The Unit left OUDEZEELE to proceed to a point 1 mile N.E. of L'ABEELE + closed by in its road all day, then bivouac for the night out in field 1 mile S.W. of POPERINGHE on POPERINGHE — L'ABEELE Rd. Sgt.	

Army Form C. 2118.

WAR DIARY
or
INTELLIGENCE SUMMARY.
(Erase heading not required.)

Instructions regarding War Diaries and Intelligence Summaries are contained in F. S. Regs., Part II. and the Staff Manual respectively. Title pages will be prepared in manuscript.

Hour, Date, Place	Summary of Events and Information	Remarks and references to Appendices
April 27th 1915. 1 mile S.W. POPERINGHE on POPERINGHE — L'ABEELE Rd.	Standing by all day awaiting orders. At 11:55 pm an order was received to send 1 Officer 1 N.C.O & 2 men with 1 motor Ambulance & 1 light ambulance to VLAMERTINGHE, for duty. E.D.E.	
April 28th 1915. From 1 mile N.E. of STEENVOORDE, km HILL 20. (Ref. map HAZEBROUCK 1cm)	Standing by. The officer with the motor ambulance evacuated 5 wounded from the Brigade at VLAMERTINGHE to C.C.S. at HM? LE BROUCK. At 12 a.m. orders were received to march at one hour's notice to its home. At 6 pm, the unit moved to its billet. E.D.E.	

WAR DIARY
or
INTELLIGENCE SUMMARY.
(Erase heading not required.)

Army Form C. 2118.

Instructions regarding War Diaries and Intelligence Summaries are contained in F.S. Regs., Part II. and the Staff Manual respectively. Title pages will be prepared in manuscript.

Hour, Date, Place	Summary of Events and Information	Remarks and references to Appendices
April 29th 1915 a farm 1 mile N. E. of STEENVOORDE near Hill 20. (Ref what HAZEBROUCK 1in.).	Left for Cross roads on WATOU - L'ABEELE Rd 1 mile NW of L'ABEELE received at 7 pm orders received to return to Billets. SD8	
April 30th 1915 farm 1 mile NE of STEENVOORDE near Hill 20.	Left Billets for Cross roads on WATOU - L'ABEELE road 1 mile NW of L'ABEELE. saw written others. At 6 p.m. proceeded to billets occupied in previous night. SD8	

[signature] Lt Col

121/5/25

May 1915

3rd Cavalry Division

No 8. Cavalry Field Ambulance

Vol VI

10/5/25

Army Form C. 2118.

WAR DIARY
~~INTELLIGENCE SUMMARY.~~
(Erase heading not required.)

Instructions regarding War Diaries and Intelligence Summaries are contained in F.S. Regs., Part II. and the Staff Manual respectively. Title pages will be prepared in manuscript.

Hour, Date, Place	Summary of Events and Information	Remarks and references to Appendices
May 1st 1915. Farm one mile NE. of STEENVOORDE near HILL 20	Left Westoutre cross roads on WATOU — L'ABEELE Rd 1 mile N.W. of L'ABEELE at 7 AM remaining there until 5·PM under orders	
May 2nd 1915. Farm one mile NE of STEENVOORDE near Hill 20	Proceeded to Brigade rendezvous & remained there from 8.30 AM until 5·PM awaiting orders. At 11·55 Dr GREEN F. admitted to Hospital & evacuated.	
May 3rd 1915. Farm one mile NE of STEENVOORDE and POINT 35	Joined Brigade at rendezvous at 6 PM & proceeded with it to POINT 35 — Ref map HAZEBROUCK 5a — on arrival there one Officer one N.C.O. 8 men and 1 motor Ambulance detailed for duty at wounded clearing station near YPRES	

Forms/C. 2118/10

Army Form C. 2118.

WAR DIARY
or
INTELLIGENCE SUMMARY.
(Erase heading not required.)

Instructions regarding War Diaries and Intelligence Summaries are contained in F.S. Regs., Part II. and the Staff Manual respectively. Title pages will be prepared in manuscript.

Hour, Date, Place	Summary of Events and Information	Remarks and references to Appendices
May 4th 1915. Point 35. Rd nr Hazebrouck	Left Point 35 at 8 AM for Windmill 3 kilometres S.W. of WATOU on the HOUTKERQUE - HERZEELE Rd arriving there about 11.30 AM	
May 5th 1915. HOUTKERQUE	Brigade laying details for trench digging. 2 Officers 1 N.C.O. & men of 2 nearest ambulances ordered to accompany them	
May 6th 1915. HOUTKERQUE	The party that accompanied trench guard returned to billets at 5 AM	

Army Form C. 2118.

WAR DIARY
or
INTELLIGENCE SUMMARY.
(Erase heading not required.)

Instructions regarding War Diaries and Intelligence
Summaries are contained in F. S. Regs., Part II.
and the Staff Manual respectively. Title pages
will be prepared in manuscript.

Hour, Date, Place	Summary of Events and Information	Remarks and references to Appendices
May 7th 1915. HOUTKERQUE & BLARINGHEM.	Unit still in same billets. Left at 3.30pm & proceeded to old billets at BLARINGHEM. Under orders to move at 3 hrs 40 min notice. S.S.²	
May 8th 1915. BLARINGHEM.	Remained in billets all day, under orders to move at 3 hrs 40 min if necessary. S.S.²	
May 9th 1915. Pt 35. (Refrat. HAZEBROUCK Ja.)	Two Officers Abc men with two motor ambulances left for YPRES, reestablished dressing Station at former posts, nr YPRES on the POPERINGHE-YPRES road. The Remainder of "A" Section moved to a joint husbandry between POPERINGHE & FORGE (West HAZEBROUCK Ja.), the three A Sections of the Cav. Field Ambs² of the Brigade were together. S.S.²	

Army Form C. 2118.

WAR DIARY
or
INTELLIGENCE SUMMARY.
(Erase heading not required.)

Instructions regarding War Diaries and Intelligence Summaries are contained in F. S. Regs., Part II. and the Staff Manual respectively. Title pages will be prepared in manuscript.

Hour, Date, Place	Summary of Events and Information	Remarks and references to Appendices
May 10th 1915. Pt 35.	Unit moved in the forenoon to Pt 35. (HAZEBROUCK Dn.) the three "A" Echelon horses in some field. S.A.E.	
May 11th 1915. Pt 35.	Unit awaited orders. S.A.E.	
May 12th 1915. Pt 35.	Lt DOWNIE formed an advanced dressing station at White Chateau on the YPRES - ZONNEBEKE road. S.A.E.	
May 13th 1915 Pt 35.	63 wounded came through its dressing stations of the Brigade Field Ambulance. S.A.D.S.	
May 14th 1915. Pt 35.	76 wounded came through its dressing stations of the Field Ambulance. S.A.E.	

Army Form C. 2118.

WAR DIARY
or
INTELLIGENCE SUMMARY.
(Erase heading not required.)

Instructions regarding War Diaries and Intelligence Summaries are contained in F. S. Regs., Part II. and the Staff Manual respectively. Title pages will be prepared in manuscript.

Hour, Date, Place	Summary of Events and Information	Remarks and references to Appendices
May 15th 1915. Pt 35.	20 wounded came into dressing station at Pt 35 Kharrift last night	Sgd ?
May 16th 1915. Pt 35.	Usual routine	Sgd ?
May 17th 1915. Pt 35.	No 1036 Pte RUTTER was evacuated to No 10. C.C.S. suffering from severe burns.	Sgd ?
May 18th 1915. Pt 35.	No. M2/020575 Dvr. WARD A.S.C. M.T. (hospital Pera created). One history ambulance return) to accompany Brigade digging party or 11 hrn.	Sgd ?
May 19th 1915. Pt 35.	Usual routine	Sgd ?

Army Form C. 2118.

WAR DIARY
or
INTELLIGENCE SUMMARY.
(Erase heading not required.)

Instructions regarding War Diaries and Intelligence Summaries are contained in F. S. Regs., Part II. and the Staff Manual respectively. Title pages will be prepared in manuscript.

Hour, Date, Place	Summary of Events and Information	Remarks and references to Appendices
May 20th 1915. Pt. 35.	General Routine. A message was received from the Brigadier as follows:— "The Brigadier wishes to thank Lt.Col. CLAYTON, OFFICERS, N.C.O's & Men of the 8th (Cavalry field) ambulance for the very good work they did during the recent action." E.D.S.	
May 21st 1915. BLARINGHEM.	The Unit received orders to proceed to their old billets at BLARINGHEM. One officer, one man & a motor ambulance were left behind to accompany the 1st Brigade. Convoy up to 1 Brigade took up billets at 9. P.M. E.D.S.	
May 23rd 1915. BLARINGHEM.	General routine. E.D.S.	

Army Form C. 2118.

WAR DIARY
or
INTELLIGENCE SUMMARY
(Erase heading not required.)

Instructions regarding War Diaries and Intelligence Summaries are contained in F.S. Regs., Part II. and the Staff Manual respectively. Title pages will be prepared in manuscript.

Hour, Date, Place	Summary of Events and Information	Remarks and references to Appendices
May 23rd 1915. BLARINGHEM.	"usual routine"	S.D.S.
May 24th 1915. BLARINGHEM.	2. A.S.C. M.T. & 1 A.S.C. M.T. reinforcements received to replace casualties.	S.D.S.
May 25th 1915. BLARINGHEM.	"usual routine"	S.D.S.
May 26th 1915. BLARINGHEM.	"usual routine". Pte. DOWNIE (private) seen from 26th — 2 gs. Lt. DEANE evacuated to No.10 C.C.S. sick	S.D.S.
May 27th 1915. BLARINGHEM.	"usual routine". Lt. HALLINAN. W.F. arrived to replace Lt. DEANE for temporary duty.	S.D.S.

WAR DIARY
or
INTELLIGENCE SUMMARY.
(Erase heading not required.)

Army Form C. 2118.

Instructions regarding War Diaries and Intelligence Summaries are contained in F. S. Regs., Part II. and the Staff Manual respectively. Title pages will be prepared in manuscript.

Hour, Date, Place	Summary of Events and Information	Remarks and references to Appendices
May 29th 1915. BLARINGHEM.	2 N.C.Os + 9 men were detailed to proceed to "B" Echelon in exchange for a corresponding number of N.C.Os & men from "B" Echelon. Sgd.	
May 29th 1915. VLAMERTINGHE.	The Unit moved to VLAMERTINGHE. The Brigade being detailed for duty in the trenches. One M.O. + 6 men were left at BLARINGHEM with 2 light wagons & equipment. Sgd.	
May 30th 1915. VLAMERTINGHE.	One M.O. one N.C.O + 3 men were detailed for duty at the advanced dressing station at ECOLE DE BIENFAISANCE. Four light ambulances with orderlies + one M.O. proceeded at dusk to collect wounded at the dressing ground of the Brigade. Sgd.	
May 31st 1915. VLAMERTINGHE.		

121/6034

June 1915 -

121/6034

3rd Cavalry Division

No 8 Cavalry Field Ambulance

Vol XLL

3rd Cavalry Division

ams

WAR DIARY
or
INTELLIGENCE SUMMARY.
(Erase heading not required.)

Army Form C. 2118.

Hour, Date, Place	Summary of Events and Information	Remarks and references to Appendices
June 1st 1915 VLAMERTINGHE	Details for collecting & taking in wounded also personnel for advanced dressing station as before.	
June 2nd 1915 VLAMERTINGHE	Details as on June 1st. Lt ELLIS who has been acting MO to 10th Royal Hussars returned to duty with Field Ambulance	
June 3rd 1915 VLAMERTINGHE	Routine details. MAJOR HAMMERTON RAMC No M/S 9116 Pte BUSHELL a.e.k. M2/01838 Pte McGINLEY J were wounded by shrapnel at advanced dressing station. The latter has been severely & favourably mentioned also by M2/019205 Pte DROUGHAN E W and M2/033525 Pte MITCHELL A removed to hospital.	
June 4 1915 VLAMERTINGHE	Details as before.	

Army Form C. 2118.

WAR DIARY
or
INTELLIGENCE SUMMARY.
(Erase heading not required.)

Instructions regarding War Diaries and Intelligence Summaries are contained in F. S. Regs., Part II. and the Staff Manual respectively. Title pages will be prepared in manuscript.

Hour, Date, Place	Summary of Events and Information	Remarks and references to Appendices
June 5th 1915. VLAMERTINGHE	Details as previous day carried out	
June 6th 1915. VLAMERTINGHE	Details as before	
June 7th 1915. VLAMERTINGHE & BLARINGHEM	The usual car, one medical officer with medical & surgical equipment accompanied troops to release remainder of unit. Left VLAMERTINGHE at 4.30 AM arriving at BLARINGHEM at 12.30 PM. Lt ELLIS and his Orderlies proceeded on leave to ENGLAND. 2nd HALLINAN transferred to Royal Horse Guards as temporary M.O.	

Army Form C. 2118.

WAR DIARY
or
INTELLIGENCE SUMMARY.
(Erase heading not required.)

Instructions regarding War Diaries and Intelligence Summaries are contained in F. S. Regs., Part II. and the Staff Manual respectively. Title pages will be prepared in manuscript.

Hour, Date, Place	Summary of Events and Information	Remarks and references to Appendices
June 8th 1915. BLARINGHEM	Ordinary employment. Inspection of waggons, harness & horses. Deficiencies noted & reported.	
June 9th 1915. BLARINGHEM	Wet morning. In cleaning up & renovating. Received 3 rgts. rough horses from B Eccm. Two other ranks proceeded on leave to ENGLAND	
June 10th 1915. BLARINGHEM	General routine. Lt Downie transferred to Artillery as R.O. to B/2nd Horse Brig. Lt HALLIMAN to act as temporary M.O. with G Battery R.H.A.	

Army Form C. 2118.

WAR DIARY
or
INTELLIGENCE SUMMARY.
(Erase heading not required.)

Hour, Date, Place	Summary of Events and Information	Remarks and references to Appendices
June 11th 1915 BLARINGHEM	General Routine	
June 12th 1915 BLARINGHEM	General Routine. Inspection of wound by Lt Col F.W. HARDY RAMC ADMS 2nd Cavalry Division. Lt ELLIS 9 Lrs & Lt Ranken returned from leave. Lt DOWNIE & Lt HALLINAN 19H reported for duty. Baths were arranged for the wounded & Every facility made & supervision of Lt HALLINAN	C

Army Form C. 2118.

WAR DIARY
or
INTELLIGENCE SUMMARY.
(Erase heading not required.)

Instructions regarding War Diaries and Intelligence Summaries are contained in F.S. Regs., Part II. and the Staff Manual respectively. Title pages will be prepared in manuscript.

Hour, Date, Place	Summary of Events and Information	Remarks and references to Appendices
June 13th 1915. BLARINGHEM	Divine Service. General Rouse. Notification received that Lt. DOWNIE granted Order of St ANNE class IV by Russian Government.	
June 14th 1915. BLARINGHEM	One officer & 4 NCOs transferred on leave to ENGLAND. General sanitary. Two officers, three 9.5" R.E. tanks FANC taken on strength. French also times light. Crows M.T. horses. 20	
June 15th 1915. BLARINGHEM	General sanitary. Horses of A Echelon inspected by ADVS	

(9 29 6) W4141—463 100,000 9/14 H W V Forms/C. 2118/10

Army Form C. 2118.

WAR DIARY
or
INTELLIGENCE SUMMARY.
(Erase heading not required.)

Instructions regarding War Diaries and Intelligence Summaries are contained in F.S. Regs., Part II. and the Staff Manual respectively. Title pages will be prepared in manuscript.

Hour, Date, Place	Summary of Events and Information	Remarks and references to Appendices
June 16th 1915 - BLARINGHEM	General Routine. Inspection of Brigade regimental billets by ADMS and Lt Col CLAYTON. No 8730 Pte Sn. AUDUS C.W. awarded to South Midland C.C's suffering from fracture of left humerus.	
June 17th 1915 - BLARINGHEM	Degree of readiness altered to 4 hours from receipt of orders. General Routine.	
June 18th 1915 - BLARINGHEM	Inspection of Brigade by Field Marshal Gen. Sir John French at 12 noon in field near ERCUS. A case reported on 14th now reported as suspected. All necessary precautions re contacts taken.	

(9 29 6) W 4141—463 100,000 9/14 H W V Forms/C. 2118/10

Army Form C. 2118.

WAR DIARY
or
INTELLIGENCE SUMMARY.
(Erase heading not required.)

Hour, Date, Place	Summary of Events and Information	Remarks and references to Appendices
June 19th 1915. BLARINGHEM.	The following appointments to form Staff took place:- Q.M.S. ARMSTRONG to be S.M. vice QSM. Andrews. S. Sgt. WHITE to be Q.M.S. Sgt. TURNER to be S. Sgt. Cpl. TATTERSALL to be Sgt. Staff	
June 20th 1915. BLARINGHEM.	General routine	
June 21st 1915 BLARINGHEM.	Lt. L. A. MORAN reported for duty from X.R.H. Was taken on the strength.	
June 22nd 1915. BLARINGHEM.	Lt. LANCE R.A.M.C. arrived from LE HAVRE was taken on the strength.	
June 23rd 1915. BLARINGHEM.	One motor ambulance was sent to X.R.H. to take Offr Cooper to Machine Gun instruction Camp.	

Army Form C. 2118.

WAR DIARY
or
INTELLIGENCE SUMMARY.
(Erase heading not required.)

Instructions regarding War Diaries and Intelligence Summaries are contained in F.S. Regs., Part II. and the Staff Manual respectively. Title pages will be prepared in manuscript.

Hour, Date, Place	Summary of Events and Information	Remarks and references to Appendices
June 24th 1915. BLARINGHEM.	The billets in the village were thoroughly cleaned out & disinfected by the Field Ambulance. Sd/S.	
June 25th 1915. BLARINGHEM.	General routine. Sd/S.	
June 26th 1915. BLARINGHEM.	General routine. Sd/S.	
June 27th 1915. BLARINGHEM.	Church routine. Sd/S.	
June 28th 1915. BLARINGHEM.	Lt. HALLINAN reports to O.C. "A" Echelon No 6 C.F.A. Pass taken off through of the unit. The Chaplain returned from leave. Sd/S.	

Army Form C. 2118.

WAR DIARY
or
INTELLIGENCE SUMMARY.
(Erase heading not required.)

Instructions regarding War Diaries and Intelligence Summaries are contained in F. S. Regs., Part II. and the Staff Manual respectively. Title pages will be prepared in manuscript.

Hour, Date, Place	Summary of Events and Information	Remarks and references to Appendices
June 29th 1915. BLARINGHEM.	General routine. Sgd.	
June 30th 1915. BLARINGHEM.	Lt. J. DOWNIE returns from leave. Lt. E.D ELLIS on furlough leave from 1st/7/15 to 8/7/15 incl. Sgd.	

Forms/C. 2118/10

121/6410

131/6410

3rd Cavalry Division

8th Cavalry Field Ambulance

Vol VIII

from 1st to 31st July 1915

amb

July 15

Army Form C. 2118.

WAR DIARY
or
INTELLIGENCE SUMMARY.
(Erase heading not required.)

Instructions regarding War Diaries and Intelligence Summaries are contained in F. S. Regs., Part II. and the Staff Manual respectively. Title pages will be prepared in manuscript.

Hour, Date, Place	Summary of Events and Information	Remarks and references to Appendices
July 1st 1915 BLARINGHEM	General Routine	
July 2nd 1915 BLARINGHEM	Under supervision of A.D.M.S. Sanitary material prepared for & above	
July 3rd 1915 BLARINGHEM	Lecture at 2.45pm by A.D.M.S. Lt. Col. Hardy. R.A.M.C. to the officers of the 8th Cavalry Brigade.	
July 4th 1915 BLARINGHEM	General Routine	
July 5th 1915 BLARINGHEM	General Routine	

Army Form C. 2118.

WAR DIARY
or
INTELLIGENCE SUMMARY.
(Erase heading not required.)

Instructions regarding War Diaries and Intelligence Summaries are contained in F. S. Regs., Part II. and the Staff Manual respectively. Title pages will be prepared in manuscript.

Hour, Date, Place	Summary of Events and Information	Remarks and references to Appendices
July 6th 1915 BLARINGHEM.	General routine	ED
July 7th 1915 BLARINGHEM.	Pte Atkinson granted 72 hours leave	ED
July 8th 1915 BLARINGHEM.	Lt E.D. Ellis returned from leave.	ED
July 9th 1915 BLARINGHEM.	General routine	ED
July 10th 1915 BLARINGHEM.	General routine	ED
July 11th 1915 BLARINGHEM.	General routine	ED

Army Form C. 2118.

WAR DIARY
or
INTELLIGENCE SUMMARY.
(Erase heading not required.)

Instructions regarding War Diaries and Intelligence Summaries are contained in F. S. Regs., Part II. and the Staff Manual respectively. Title pages will be prepared in manuscript.

Hour, Date, Place	Summary of Events and Information	Remarks and references to Appendices
July 12th 1915. BLARINGHEM.	General routine	
July 13th 1915. BLARINGHEM.	General routine	
July 14th 1915. BLARINGHEM.	Major HILL. O.C. A.S.C. III Cav. Div. inspected the transport of 76 Bonk at 10 a.m.	
July 15th 1915. BLARINGHEM.	General routine.	
July 16th 1915. BLARINGHEM.	General routine.	

Army Form C. 2118.

WAR DIARY
or
INTELLIGENCE SUMMARY.
(Erase heading not required.)

Hour, Date, Place	Summary of Events and Information	Remarks and references to Appendices
17th July 1915. BLARINGHEM	General Routine	
18th July 1915. BLARINGHEM	General Routine. Lt LANCE reported for duty to ADMS 3rd Division. Veterinary Officer attached to this unit	
19th July 1915. BLARINGHEM	Inspection of B Echelon transport by D.C. A.S.C. MAJOR HILLS	
20th July 1915. BLARINGHEM	General Routine	
21st July 1915. BLARINGHEM	General Routine	

Army Form C. 2118.

WAR DIARY
or
INTELLIGENCE SUMMARY.
(Erase heading not required.)

Instructions regarding War Diaries and Intelligence Summaries are contained in F.S. Regs., Part II. and the Staff Manual respectively. Title pages will be prepared in manuscript.

Hour, Date, Place	Summary of Events and Information	Remarks and references to Appendices
22nd July 1915. BLARINGHEM	Capt HOBBS returned from leave. Brig.Nl. Ly. Nl. Army Nl. Thorpe & Cast- Ly G.O.C. 3rd C.D.	
23rd July 1915. BLARINGHEM	General Routine Lt MORAN transferred from B to A Squadron	
24th July 1915. BLARINGHEM	General Routine	
25th July 1915. BLARINGHEM	General Routine	

Army Form C. 2118.

WAR DIARY
or
INTELLIGENCE SUMMARY.
(Erase heading not required.)

Instructions regarding War Diaries and Intelligence Summaries are contained in F.S. Regs., Part II. and the Staff Manual respectively. Title pages will be prepared in manuscript.

Hour, Date, Place	Summary of Events and Information	Remarks and references to Appendices
26 July 1915 BLARINGHEM	General Routine	
27 July 1915 BLARINGHEM	General Routine	
28 July 1915 BLARINGHEM	B.17 A cars sent for renovation 9 repairs to F.A.W.U. wagons DDMS Cavalry Corps, Surg. Gen. O'KEEFE inspected lines.	
29 July 1915 BLARINGHEM	General Routine 8 of our ADMS embark cars sent to rent for duty	

WAR DIARY
or
INTELLIGENCE SUMMARY.
(Erase heading not required.)

Army Form C. 2118.

Hour, Date, Place	Summary of Events and Information	Remarks and references to Appendices
30 July 1918 BLARINGHEM	Gave men exercises with B Section for morning duty	
31st July 1918 BLARINGHEM	MAJOR HAMMERTON being sent to Reliefs for duty. Capt HOBBS engineer by staff from hospital. Eight eighth draught horses received	

121/6753

3rd Cavalry Sworin

No 8. Cavy: Field Ambulance
Int IX
August 15.

Aug '15

WAR DIARY
or
INTELLIGENCE SUMMARY.
(Erase heading not required.)

Army Form C. 2118.

Hour, Date, Place	Summary of Events and Information	Remarks and references to Appendices
Aug 1st 1915. BLARINGHEM	Cap.t HOBBS evacuates to 2012 C Clearing Stn. HAZEBROUCK Cas 1115. returned from workshop 20	
Aug 2nd 1915 BLARINGHEM	Lt DOWNIE one N.C.O. 2 privates RAMC and 2 MT drivers proceeds to ELVERDINGHE with divisional trench-digging party. Lt HALLINAN reported for temporary duty with B Section. Cas 1110 returned from workshop 20. Sgt Zigtboangh horses transferred from A & B Section 20. Evening Routine	
Aug 3rd 1915 BLARINGHEM		

Army Form C. 2118.

WAR DIARY
or
INTELLIGENCE SUMMARY.
(Erase heading not required.)

Instructions regarding War Diaries and Intelligence Summaries are contained in F.S. Regs., Part II. and the Staff Manual respectively. Title pages will be prepared in manuscript.

Hour, Date, Place	Summary of Events and Information	Remarks and references to Appendices
Aug 3rd 1915 BLARINGHEM	Trench digging partly returned 2)	
Aug 4th 1915 BLARINGHEM & PETIGNY	A Echelon removed from BLARINGHEM to farm house at PETIGNY. Billets found to be unsanitary & insuitable for the working of the units $)	
Aug 4th 1915 PETIGNY	Special authorization paid to Divisition on the outlook for suitable Billets LD	

(9 29 6) W 4141—463 100,000 9/14 H W V Forms/C. 2118/10

Army Form C. 2118.

WAR DIARY
or
INTELLIGENCE SUMMARY.
(Erase heading not required.)

Instructions regarding War Diaries and Intelligence Summaries are contained in F. S. Regs., Part II. and the Staff Manual respectively. Title pages will be prepared in manuscript.

Hour, Date, Place	Summary of Events and Information	Remarks and references to Appendices
Aug 8th 1915 PETIGNY	General Routine. Lt Col CLAYTON SMO inspected stretcher bearers ESSEX YEO. 2D	
Aug 9th 1915 PETIGNY	General Routine. M/D/785·05 Dr J.E. CREER No A S C reported for duty. Lt Col CLAYTON SMO inspected stretcher bearers R.H.G. 2D	
Aug 10th 1915 PETIGNY & BOMY	Lt Col CLAYTON SMO inspected stretcher bearers 10th R Gee Hussars. Suitable billets having been found the A Echelon removed to BOMY. 2D	

WAR DIARY
or
INTELLIGENCE SUMMARY.
(Erase heading not required.)

Army Form C. 2118.

Instructions regarding War Diaries and Intelligence Summaries are contained in F.S. Regs., Part II. and the Staff Manual respectively. Title pages will be prepared in manuscript.

Hour, Date, Place	Summary of Events and Information	Remarks and references to Appendices
Aug 11th 1915. B O M Y	General railway work	
Aug 12th 1915. B O M Y	General Routine	
Aug 13th 1915. B O M Y	Lt ELLIS one NCO 2 privates RAMC 2 drivers ASC no 101 proceeded to ARMENTIERES with horses dug out party. Lt MORAN took over duties of MO to 10th Bgde Hussars in place of CAPT O'KELLY who went with party from the Regiment.	

Army Form C. 2118.

WAR DIARY
or
INTELLIGENCE SUMMARY.
(Erase heading not required.)

Instructions regarding War Diaries and Intelligence Summaries are contained in F. S. Regs., Part II. and the Staff Manual respectively. Title pages will be prepared in manuscript.

Hour, Date, Place	Summary of Events and Information	Remarks and references to Appendices
Aug 14th 1915 BOMY	L/Col CLAYTON proceeded on leave to ENGLAND. Corpl VARLEY retained to R.H.Q. for temporary duty	
Aug 15th 1915 BOMY	General Routine, M.A.S.C. 4th reinforcement joined unit	2D 2D
Aug 16th 1915 BOMY	Sergt TATTERSALL transferred to B Echelon for temporary duty	2D
Aug 17th 1915 BOMY	General Routine. Motor Cycle sent to workshop for repairs	2D

Army Form C. 2118.

WAR DIARY
or
INTELLIGENCE SUMMARY.
(Erase heading not required.)

Instructions regarding War Diaries and Intelligence Summaries are contained in F. S. Regs., Part II. and the Staff Manual respectively. Title pages will be prepared in manuscript.

Hour, Date, Place	Summary of Events and Information	Remarks and references to Appendices
Aug 18th 1915. BOMY	One RAMC reinforcement arrives 2D	
Aug 19th 1915. BOMY	General Routine 2D	
Aug 20th 1915. BOMY	General Routine 2D	
Aug 21st 1915. BOMY	Lt MORAN has this rank RAMC & two drivers ASC ND proceeds to ARMENTIERES to relieve similar rigging party. Lt HALLINAN transferred from SCFA to 6 CFA 2D	

Army Form C. 2118.

WAR DIARY
or
INTELLIGENCE SUMMARY.
(Erase heading not required.)

Instructions regarding War Diaries and Intelligence Summaries are contained in F.S. Regs., Part II. and the Staff Manual respectively. Title pages will be prepared in manuscript.

Hour, Date, Place	Summary of Events and Information	Remarks and references to Appendices
Aug 22nd 1915. BOMY	General Routine.	
Aug 23rd 1915. BOMY	Lt Col CLAYTON returned from leave.	
Aug 24th 1915. BOMY	Lt ELLIS attached to Blackenford. General Routine.	
Aug 25th 1915. BOMY	General Routine.	
Aug 26th 1915. BOMY	General Routine.	

(9 29 6) W 4141—463 100,000 9/14 H W V Forms/C. 2118/10

Army Form C. 2118.

WAR DIARY
or
INTELLIGENCE SUMMARY.

(Erase heading not required.)

Instructions regarding War Diaries and Intelligence Summaries are contained in F. S. Regs., Part II. and the Staff Manual respectively. Title pages will be prepared in manuscript.

Hour, Date, Place	Summary of Events and Information	Remarks and references to Appendices
Aug 24th 1915 BOMY	General Routine ʒɒ	
Aug 28th 1915 BOMY	General Routine ʒɒ	
Aug 29th 1915 BOMY	General Routine ʒɒ	
Aug 30th 1915 BOMY	General Routine ʒɒ	
Aug 31st 1915 BOMY	General Routine ʒɒ	

121/7050.

3rd Cavalry Division

8th Cavy: Field Ambulance

Vol X

Sep. 15

Sep/15

Army Form C. 2118

WAR DIARY
or
INTELLIGENCE SUMMARY.
(Erase heading not required.)

Instructions regarding War Diaries and Intelligence Summaries are contained in F. S. Regs., Part II. and the Staff Manual respectively. Title pages will be prepared in manuscript.

Place	Date	Hour	Summary of Events and Information	Remarks and references to Appendices
Bony	Sep 15		General Routine 20	
Bony	2/9/15		General Routine 20	
Bony	3/9/15		General Routine 20	
Bony	4/9/15		French diggers party returned from ARMENTIERES 20	
Bony	5/9/15		General Routine 20	
Bony	6/9/15		General Routine 20	
Bony	7/9/15		2 wounded gunners in A.S.C. returned from B.Z. Gbes. 2.8 No. ? laws for forage cart	

WAR DIARY
or
INTELLIGENCE SUMMARY.

(Erase heading not required.)

Army Form C. 2118

Instructions regarding War Diaries and Intelligence Summaries are contained in F. S. Regs., Part II. and the Staff Manual respectively. Title pages will be prepared in manuscript.

Place	Date	Hour	Summary of Events and Information	Remarks and references to Appendices
BOMY	8/9/15		Sir draught those received from B Echelon new Rifles with eyes cleaned from workshop	
BOMY	9/9/15		Pte Wright dies at night. Horse received to Nr. 20 M.V. section	
BOMY	10/9/15		Swan horse transferred from B Echelon for casualty at B.C. 6 coy	
BOMY	11/9/15		Major F.C. Timmins C.F reported for duty	
BOMY	12/9/15		Equine Routine	
BOMY	13/9/15		Equine Routine	

WAR DIARY
or
INTELLIGENCE SUMMARY.

(Erase heading not required.)

Army Form C. 2118

Place	Date	Hour	Summary of Events and Information	Remarks and references to Appendices
BOMY	14/9/15		Brigade in full marching order	
BOMY	15/9/15		CAPTN YATES R.A.M.C. reporting for duty	
BOMY	16/9/15		General Routine	
BOMY	17/9/15		Took part in inspection manoeuvres with Brigade	
BOMY	18/9/15		General Routine	
BOMY	19/9/15		General Routine	
BOMY	20/9/15		CAPTN A L YATES left for duty with 15th Div. MAJOR TIMMINS Ct Asst for duty with 4th Cav. Brigade	

WAR DIARY
or
INTELLIGENCE SUMMARY.
(Erase heading not required.)

Army Form C. 2118

Place	Date	Hour	Summary of Events and Information	Remarks and references to Appendices
BOMY	14/9/15		Brigade in full marching order	
BOMY	15/9/15		CAPT A YATES RAMC reported for duty	
BOMY	16/9/15		Brigade in full marching order	
BOMY	17/9/15		Left roads in lieu of manoeuvre ar Brigade	
BOMY	18/9/15		Ennui et Routine	
BOMY	19/9/15		Ennui et Routine	
BOMY	20/9/15		CAPT AL YATES left for duty with 15 & Div. MAJOR TIMMINS Cd. Bgde for duty with 4th Cav. Brigade	

Army Form C. 2118

WAR DIARY
or
INTELLIGENCE SUMMARY.
(Erase heading not required.)

Place	Date	Hour	Summary of Events and Information	Remarks and references to Appendices
BOMY	20/9/15	6-30pm	Received orders from Brigade Headquarters for the Field Amb. to rendezvous at 1-30pm the following day at the cross roads 1/2 mile North of F.n FONTAINE-LEZ-HERMANS. Marching Order. SO&D	
BOMY	21/9/15	11-30am	Left BOMY via CUHEM and T.LECHIN for rendezvous at 1/2 mile North of F.n FONTAINE-LEZ-HERMANS ref. map HAZEBROUCK 100,000. Arrived at rendez-vous at 1-30 P.M. remained here until 6 P.M. when the Field Ambulance was ordered to proceed to LABEUVRIERE arrived there. 11-30 P.M. SO&D	
LABEUVRIERE	22/9/15		Ordered to Stand-by at 2 hours notice. Formed A. ECHELON. A. ECHELON I and A. ECHELON II. A. ECHELON I to consist of 2 Officers 1 N.C.O and 5 men R.A.M.C. 1 N.C.O and 2 men R.A.M.C. H.T. all mounted on horses this Echelon the Field horse horsed with extra strong and fresh horses. To equipment consists of 2 Medical Companions, 6 Surgical Haversacks, 6 Haversacks with Field Dressings, 6 Water Bottles, each man and horse carries Iron Rations. A. ECHELON II consists of the remainder of the Field Ambulance. A. ECHELON. A. ECHELON I fully equipped ready to keep up with the Cavalry. MAJOR HAMMERTON arrived at 6 P.m. SO&D and A. ECHELON. SO&D	
LABEUVRIERE	23/9/15		Standing by at 2 hours notice. Notice reduced to 1/2 hour. SO&D	

Army Form C. 2118

WAR DIARY
of
INTELLIGENCE SUMMARY.
(Erase heading not required.)

Instructions regarding War Diaries and Intelligence Summaries are contained in F. S. Regs., Part II. and the Staff Manual respectively. Title pages will be prepared in manuscript.

Place	Date	Hour	Summary of Events and Information	Remarks and references to Appendices
LABEUVRIERE	24/9/15	5-30 A.M.	Standing by at ½ hrs notice. Received orders to be ready to move the following day at 5-30 A.M. GOYD.	
LABEUVRIERE	25/9/15	5-30 A.M.	Ready to move. At 8-30 A.M. A.ECHELON. I received orders to proceed to Brigade Rendezvous at the B. of BOIS DES DAMES 1½ mp. HAZEBROUCK. 1½ 000 A.ECHELON. to proceed to LABUISSIERE and report to Divisional Headquarters. A.ECHELON.I proceeded to [illeg.] Brigade to a point ½ mile W of VERMELLES and Bivouaced. A.ECHELON.II proceeded with the remainder of the A.ECHELONS II to NOEUX-LES-MINES, reales 2 toms and then Proceeded to NOYELLES-LEZ-VERMELLES. and bivouaced for the night. GOYD.	
NOYELLES-LEZ-VERMELLES	26/9/15		Stood by until NOON. A.ECHELON II were ordered back to NOEUX-LES-MINES. Brigade ordered up to Trenches at 6. P.M. GOYD.	
NOYELLES-LEZ-VERMELLES	27/9/15	12.30A.M.	Collected 8 wounded men of ROYAL HORSE GUARDS who were proceeding up to the Trenches. GOYD.	
"	"	3 A.M.	Brigade again ordered to Trenches. Field Ambulance found Dressing Station at PHILOSOPHE at Cross roads ½ mile S.W. of VERMELLES. (BETHUNE MAP Contoured Sheet 36 c NW ½ 10000.) GOYD.	

WAR DIARY
or
INTELLIGENCE SUMMARY.
(Erase heading not required.)

Army Form C. 2118

Place	Date	Hour	Summary of Events and Information	Remarks and references to Appendices
PHILOSOPHE	27/9/15		Opened Dressing Station and formed Advanced Dressing Station at FOSSE NO. 7. BETHUNE- LENS ROAD. m/charge 1 N.C.O. and 2 men. Captain B. D. Ellis reported for duty. G/1/21.	
do	do	5.30 PM	Sent 1 Trained Officer, 12 Stretcher Bearers and 6 Light Ambulance Wagons to collect wounded at Cross road G.34.d.10.5. BETHUNE MAP Central Shed two. Collected 12 wounded of our Brigade and 30 Infantry wounded. G/1/21	
do	do	8.30 PM	Captain J. DOWNIE wounded. G.S. wound of Right forearm and fractured Ulna. No 85 Private H. HEPWORTH. KILLED. The O.C. Lieut. Col. W.K. CLAYTON badly shaken by the same shell. G/1/21. Receiving slightly wounded cases all day at the Dressing Station. Captain Ellis and 5 R.H.9 men for duty Evra.	
PHILOSOPHE	28/9/15		Lieut Moran led for duty to the 16th R. Hussars, Lieut. Bannerman and Lieut. Wills and Douglas reported from 1st Car. Amb. and the letter two from 2nd Car. Am. for duty.	
do	28/9/15		2 M.O's, 12 Stretcher Bearers and 6 Light Ambulance Wagons sent to L.O.O.S. to collect wounded, collected all wounded from our Brigade also several to cellars in L.O.O.S. (who had been wounded)	
do	28/9/15	5.3 PM	found many wounded who had laid for five days in the cellars, Transported at 3 A.M. 29/9/15. Total number of wounded who passed through Dressing Station from 27/9 to 29/9/15 (3 A.M.) Cavalry Officers 6. O.R's Ranks 21. Infantry Officers 119. O.R's Ranks 150. Total 2nd Cav Brigade turned here for Trenches 3.A.M. Evra	

Army Form C. 2118

WAR DIARY
or
INTELLIGENCE SUMMARY.
(Erase heading not required.)

Instructions regarding War Diaries and Intelligence Summaries are contained in F. S. Regs., Part II. and the Staff Manual respectively. Title pages will be prepared in manuscript.

Place	Date	Hour	Summary of Events and Information	Remarks and references to Appendices
PHILOSOPHE	29/9/15	5 A.M.	Orders to send billeting party to Officers at LABUISSIERE r/f Maps BETHUNE. Arrival at 6.30 A.M. Sick Ambulance left for LABEUVRIERE at 8.30 A.M. arrived 1.30 P.M. Headquarters L'HOSPICE LIEUTS. BANNERMAN. WILLS and DOUGLAS returns to their units GHQ.	
LABEUVRIERE	30.9.		Standing by to leave notice. Checked equipment and replenished stores. CAPTAIN BENSON, LIEUT. CLARKE and LIEUT. LUMB reports for duty. Esort	

Meleyen Clayton C.Col
O/C 8 Can Bde Field Amb

2353 Wt. W2344/1454 700,000 5/15 D. D. & L. A.D.S.S./Forms/C. 2118.

|2|/7449

3rd Cavalry Division

8th Cav. Bde.

Oct -'15

Vol XI

Oct 9/15

Army Form C. 2118

WAR DIARY
or
INTELLIGENCE SUMMARY.
(Erase heading not required.)

Instructions regarding War Diaries and Intelligence Summaries are contained in F. S. Regs., Part II. and the Staff Manual respectively. Title pages will be prepared in manuscript.

Place	Date	Hour	Summary of Events and Information	Remarks and references to Appendices
LABEUVRIERE	1/10/15		Standing by. LIEUT. CLARKE sent to 10 R. HUSSARS for duty to replace LIEUT. MORAN. LIEUT. MORAN reports to the unit for duty. WOLSLEY MOTOR AMBULANCE issued. E.o.d.	
LABEUVRIERE	2/10/15		Standing by. Othy orders morning's E.o.d.	
LABEUVRIERE	3/10/15	10 A.M.	Billeting party orders to head Staff Captain at LOZINGHEM at 11·15 A.M.	
do		11 A.M.	Received orders to proceed to LOZINGHEM, and to be on railway siding at LAPUGNOY by 12·15 P.M. arrived at LOZINGHEM at 1·20 P.M. and received orders to proceed to BURBURE arrived at 2·30 P.M. Billets on ROAD to mile S of BURBURE E.o.d.	
BURBURE	4/10/15		Standing by to have rifles Escort Capt. ELLIS orders to proceed to ENGLAND man autony.	
do	5/10/15		Standing by. D.D.M.S. Cavalry Corps E.o.d.	
do			Standing by to move this. 3. O.R. reinforcement received. 2 to use G.S. horses received to replace full horse G.S. Surgeon Pony's Driver overcoat. E.o.d.	
do	6/10/15		3 Reinforcement R.A.M.C. received, posted to "A" Echelon. Standing by. E.o.d.	
do	7/10/15		Standing by. E.o.d.	
do	8/10/15		Standing by. E.o.d.	
do	9/10/15		Standing by. Opened DETENTION WARD for Slight cases. E.o.d.	
do	10/10/15		Standing by 3 L.O. HORSES received.	

Army Form C. 2118.

WAR DIARY
or
INTELLIGENCE SUMMARY.

(Erase heading not required.)

Instructions regarding War Diaries and Intelligence Summaries are contained in F. S. Regs., Part II. and the Staff Manual respectively. Title pages will be prepared in manuscript.

Place	Date	Hour	Summary of Events and Information	Remarks and references to Appendices
BURBURE	11/10/15		Standing By. Contd.	
BURBURE	12/10/15		Standing By Contd.	
BURBURE	13/10/15		5 LIGHT DRAUGHT HORSES and 6 "B" ECHELON. DRIVER GANLEY N°. 96. R.A.M.C. H.T. reported for duty. Standing By. Contd.	
BURBURE	14/10/15		Standing by. Received instructions from A.D.M.S. 3RD. CAV. DIV. to hire on charge a FORAGE CART in place of G.S. WAGON. To lock G.S. WAGON to be delivered to TRANSPORT OFFICER 2 CAV. BGE. Contd.	
BURBURE	15/10/15		Standing by. Contd.	
BURBURE	16/10/15		Standing by Contd.	
BURBURE	17/10/15		1 RIDING HORSE reinforcement arrived. 16 CASES of SCABIES from ESSEX YEO, mounted DETENTION WARD. and evacuated to N°1 ~~CANADIAN~~ CANADIAN. C.C.S. Contd.	
BURBURE	18/10/15		Orders received from A.D.M.S. 3RD. CAV. DIV. for "B" ECHELON to join "A" ECHELON afterwards countermanded. Contd.	
do.	do	10 P.M.	Received orders from BDE. HQS. that N°1 FIELD AMB. must be ready to move at 9 A.M. on the 19/10/15 Contd.	
BURBURE	19/10/15	8:45 A.M.	Received orders from BDE. HQS. that N°1 FIELD AMB. to rendezvous at 9.15 A.M. on the Contd.	

WAR DIARY
or
INTELLIGENCE SUMMARY

(Erase heading not required.)

Army Form C. 2118

Instructions regarding War Diaries and Intelligence Summaries are contained in F. S. Regs., Part II. and the Staff Manual respectively. Title pages will be prepared in manuscript.

Place	Date	Hour	Summary of Events and Information	Remarks and references to Appendices
BURBURE	19/15	8.45 AM	BELLERY — HURIONVILLE ROAD, HEAD OF COLUMN 1/2 L. EAST OF CROSS ROADS 1/2 MILE EAST OF BELLERY (REF. MAP. HAZEBROUCK 5A (10000.)): procured hwy. AMETTES. NEDON. FONTAINE — LES. HERMANS. PALFART. BEAUMETZ-LES-AIRE to RECLINGHEM, ordered to billet there the night, men in billets. CAPTAIN J. H. GROVE-WHITE reports for duty, was temporarily attached to R.H.G.ds Gords.	
RECLINGHEM	20/10		Standing by. Received orders to move to Permanent Billets at BEAUMETZ-LES-AIRE (My. MAP. HAZEBROUCK 5A (10000.)) on the 21st and to be the f temporary Bulls. 4 11. AM. Gords.	
RECLINGHEM	21/10		FLD. AMB. moved off at 9.30 AM. arrived BEAUMETZ-LES-AIRE at 10-30 AM. MEN billeted in BARNS. HORSES placed under cover. Boots.	
BEAUMETZ -LES-AIRE.	22/10		LIEUT. COL. W. K. CLAYTON. appointed Temporary A.D.M.S. 2nd CAV. DIV. during the absence of LIEUT COL. HARDY. on leave. "B" ECHELON. joined up with "A" ECHELON. and were also billets in BARNS. and HORSES placed under cover. This VILLAGE is very unsatisfactory, it being impossible to find a form suitable for use as a DETENTION WARD. all Cross Roads Picket in BDE. Area is to be evacuated to a C.C.S. leading to VILLAGE Rd. CAPT. GROVE WHITE rejoined FLD. AMB. CAPT. MORAN granted 14 DAYS leave to ENGLAND. Gord.	

2353 Wt. W3544/1454 700,000 5/15 D. D. & L. A.D.S.S./Forms/C. 2118.

Army Form C.2118

WAR DIARY
or
INTELLIGENCE SUMMARY.
(Erase heading not required.)

Instructions regarding War Diaries and Intelligence Summaries are contained in F. S. Regs., Part II. and the Staff Manual respectively. Title pages will be prepared in manuscript.

Place	Date	Hour	Summary of Events and Information	Remarks and references to Appendices
BEAUMETZ -LES-AIRE	23/10/15		Orderlies equipment. Wagons re. Evacuated 15 cases of SCABIES from ESSEX.YEO. to N°1 CANADIAN.C.C.S. 80701.	
BEAUMETZ -LES-AIRE	24/10/15		DIVINE SERVICE by REV. GIBBS held in School at 6 P.M. 80701	
BEAUMETZ -LES-AIRE	25/10/15		General Routine 80701	
BEAUMETZ -LES-AIRE	26/10/15		General Routine 80701	
BEAUMETZ -LES-AIRE	27/10/15		3 N.C.O's re-engaged for to Reserve 1/2 hour or 4 years. Received or Reinforcement A.S.C. M.T.. General Routine 80701	
BEAUMETZ -LES-AIRE	28/10/15		5 MEN 1 Unit. were sent to A.S.C. Supply Column 3rd CAV.DIV. to be listed as to their fitness to transfer as MECHANICS to A.S.C. General Routine, 80701.	
BEAUMETZ -LES-AIRE	29/10/15		1 L.D. HORSE reinforcement. General Routine 80701.	

2353 Wt W.;541/1154 700,000 5/15 D. D. & L. A.D.S.S./Forms/C. 2118.

Army Form C2118

WAR DIARY
or
INTELLIGENCE SUMMARY.
(Erase heading not required.)

Instructions regarding War Diaries and Intelligence Summaries are contained in F.S. Regs., Part II. and the Staff Manual respectively. Title pages will be prepared in manuscript.

Place	Date	Hour	Summary of Events and Information	Remarks and references to Appendices
BEAUMETZ-LES-AIRE	30/15	12:15	Handed over to Lieut G.S. WAGON M.C. 10. Surplus to establishment to TRANSPORT OFFICER 8 CAV. BGE. General Routine good.	
BEAUMETZ-LES-AIRE	31/15	10	LIEUT. COLONEL W.K. CLAYTON on leave to ENGLAND. 1 R.H. and I.L.D. Horse cast. Surplus to establishment. Received orders from A.D.M.S. 3rd CAV.DIV. for A' ECHELON to proceed to proceed with DIVISIONAL TRENCH DIGGING PARTY and take on MEDICAL CHARGE of DIVISION. ADVANCE PARTY consisting of 1 OFFICER i/n.c.o and 3 men with 1 MOTOR AMBULANCE and sufficient equipment to [illegible] RENDEZ-VOUS at ENGUINGATTE at 12 noon on NOV. 1st. CAPTAIN A.H. BENSON attached temporarily to ESSEX YEOMANRY as MEDICAL OFFICER. good.	

[signature] Major, R.A.M.C.

[stamp: 3rd CAVALRY FIELD AMBULANCE]

A.D.S.S./Forms/C. 2118.

3rd Cavalry Division

121/7636

No. 8 Cav. 9? Amals.

Nov. 1915

XII
Vol.

Nov 1915

Army Form C. 2118.

WAR DIARY
or
INTELLIGENCE SUMMARY.

(Erase heading not required.)

Instructions regarding War Diaries and Intelligence Summaries are contained in F. S. Regs., Part II. and the Staff Manual respectively. Title pages will be prepared in manuscript.

No. ...... Date 30/8/15
N? 8 CAVALRY FIELD AMBULANCE

Place	Date	Hour	Summary of Events and Information	Remarks and references to Appendices
BEAUMETZ-LES-AIRE	1/9/15		Received orders from A.D.M.S. 3rd Cav. Div. for "A" Echelon consisting of 2 officers, 40 O. Ranks together with 3 Light Ambulances, 2 Motor Ambulances and supplies & equipment to proceed to ST LEGER the following morning at 9 A.M. Advance Party left for ST LEGER. (Ry. Map HAZEBROUCK 5A 1/100000). Received A.S.C. H.T. reinforcement. G.O.D.	
BEAUMETZ-LES-AIRE	2/9/15		"A" Echelon moved off at 9 A.M. "B" Echelon consisting of remainder of unit left behind at BEAUMETZ-LES-AIRE under the command of CAPT. GROVE-WHITE.	
ST LEGER	2/9/15	2 P.M.	"A" Echelon arrived at ST LEGER, found the place unsuitable for establishing a Detention Ward. Moved on to LYNDE (ref. map HAZEBROUCK 5A 1/100000) Visited 6", 7" & 8" Brigade digging parties and arranged for the Medical Inspection of their Sick. G.O.D.	
LYNDE	3/9/15		Visited all the Brigades. Sent 1 man to R.H.G. and 16 Essex Yeomanry for Sunday augert duties. G.O.D.	
LYNDE	4/9/15		Orderly Officer visited the Brigades & visited the sick. G.O.D.	
LYNDE	5/9/15		The 6" & 7" Brigades returned to their permanent billeting areas, leaving the 8" Brigade at WALLON CAPPEL. Orderly Officer visiting	

WAR DIARY or INTELLIGENCE SUMMARY

Army Form C. 2118.

Place	Date	Hour	Summary of Events and Information	Remarks and references to Appendices
LYNDE	5/7		The Sick. Parade.	
LYNDE	6/7		Usual routine. Orderly Officer visited BRIGADE & saw sick. Parade.	
LYNDE	7/7		Lieut. Col. W.K. CLAYTON R.A.M.C. returned from leave in England. Capt. L.A. MORAN R.A.M.C. also " " " " Brigade visited by Orderly Officer. Parade.	
LYNDE	8/7		Received orders from A.D.M.S. 3rd CAV. DIV. to proceed on the 9th to OUDERDOM for medical duties with III CAVALRY DIVISIONAL DIGGING PARTY. Orderly Officer visited BRIGADE, usual routine Parade.	
LYNDE	9/7		"A" Echelon left LYNDE for OUDERDOM (Reg. Map. HAZEBROUCK 5A 7000) at 10-30 AM. arrived OUDERDOM 4-30 PM and waited for Orders. Sords	
OUDERDOM	9/7	6 PM	Received orders to send one Officer and 1 N.C.O. and 4 men with one MOTOR AMBULANCE and a Pr (Previous) of Medical and Surgical Equipment to 12 HUTS on 2 VLAMERTINGE - RENINGHELST ROAD and to report to O.C. DIGGING PARTY for duty. The remainder of "A" Echelon ordered to return to LYNDE. When they arrived at 2 AM. 10/7. Sords	
LYNDE	10/7		Received orders from A.D.M.S. 3rd CAV. DIV. to send an advanced MOTOR AMBULANCE to the Digging Party at VLAMERTINGE. also to for the remainder of "A" ECHELON will be encamped. Sords	

Army Form C. 2118

WAR DIARY
or
INTELLIGENCE SUMMARY

(Erase heading not required.)

Instructions regarding War Diaries and Intelligence Summaries are contained in F.S. Regs., Part II. and the Staff Manual respectively. Title Pages will be prepared in manuscript.

Place	Date	Hour	Summary of Events and Information	Remarks and references to Appendices
LYNDE	10/4/15		exception. 1 One Officer, 1 N.C.O. and 2 MEN. which were to be left behind and the Digging Party at WALLON CAPPEL, to proceed to BEAUMETZ-LES-AIRE (Ref. map HAZEBROUCK 5ᴬ) Received orders from A.D.M.S. 3ʳᵈ CAV.DIV. to furnish a Detachment from the FIELD AMBULANCE for the formation of a new FIELD AMBULANCE for duty with the new Dismounted Division.	B.M.Y.
BEAUMETZ-LES-AIRE	11/4/15		MAJOR G H L HAMMERTON. proceeded on 7 days leave to ENGLAND. General Routine Ordrs.	
BEAUMETZ-LES-AIRE	12/4/15		General Routine Ordrs.	
BEAUMETZ-LES-AIRE	13/4/15		General Routine Ordrs.	
BEAUMETZ-LES-AIRE	14/4/15		General Routine Ordrs.	
BEAUMETZ-LES-AIRE	15/4/15		Received orders from H.Q. 8ᵗʰ CAV.BRIGADE to proceed to new Billeting area on the 17/4/15. G.M.O.	
BEAUMETZ-LES-AIRE	16/4/15		General Routine. LT COL. W. K. CLAYTON. A.D.M.S. 3ʳᵈ CAV.DIV. during the absence of	

Army Form C. 2118

WAR DIARY
or
INTELLIGENCE SUMMARY
(Erase heading not required.)

Instructions regarding War Diaries and Intelligence Summaries are contained in F.S. Regs., Part II. and the Staff Manual respectively. Title Pages will be prepared in manuscript.

Place	Date	Hour	Summary of Events and Information	Remarks and references to Appendices
BEAUMETZ-LES-AIRE	16/4/15		Absence of LT. COL. PRYNNE on leave to ENGLAND. GORD.	
BEAUMETZ-LES-AIRE	17/4/15		FIELD AMBULANCE left BEAUMETZ-LES-AIRE at 8-45 A.M. and passed through FRUGES – FAUQUEMBERGUES at 10-30 A.M. arrived RIMBOVAL at 1 P.M. (Ry. hops. ARRAS Strong). and proceeded to other Billets. Left 1 N.C.O. and 5 MEN to VLAMERTINGE. (w/ hops. HAZEBROUCK 5 "A"). GORD.	
RIMBOVAL	18/4/15		Unpacking equipment. opened detailed work. Got no Work and Regiments of Brigade. GORD.	
RIMBOVAL	19/4/15		MAJOR G.H. HAMMERTON returns from leave to ENGLAND. CAPT. L.A. WEDDERBURN reported for duty. General Routine. GORD.	
RIMBOVAL	20/4/15		General Routine. GORD.	
RIMBOVAL	21/4/15		General Routine. GORD.	
RIMBOVAL	22/4/15		General Routine. GORD.	
RIMBOVAL	23/4/15		Notified of Inspection of this CAV. FIELD AMB. by D.D.M.S. CAV. CORPS. on 25/4/15. DIGGING PARTY returned from VLAMERTINGES. returned. GORD.	

Army Form C. 2118

WAR DIARY
or
INTELLIGENCE SUMMARY
(Erase heading not required.)

Place	Date	Hour	Summary of Events and Information	Remarks and references to Appendices
RIMBOVAL	24/1/15		General Routine Orders.	
RIMBOVAL	25/1/15		Inspection of new unit No. 12 C.F.A. by D.D.M.S. Cav. Corps. Capt. La Moran took on Medical Charge of X R. Hussars Temporily in Capt. J. Clarke's absence in England. General Routine Orders.	
RIMBOVAL	26/1/15		Capt. J.H. Grove - White on leave to ENGLAND. General Routine Orders.	
RIMBOVAL	27/1/15		General Routine Orders.	
RIMBOVAL	28/1/15		1 A.S.C. M.T. nunfreund received. General Routine Orders. 18 cases of Scabies sent to DIVISIONAL REST STATION from Reg'ts of BRIGADE.	
RIMBOVAL	29/1/15		1 R.A.M.C. nunfreund received. General Routine Orders.	
RIMBOVAL	30/1/15		General Routine Orders.	

Lieut. Col. R.A.M.C.
O.C. 8th C.F.A.

8th Cav. P. Ams.

Dec.
Vol XIII

FI 107/1

Dec 1915

WAR DIARY or INTELLIGENCE SUMMARY

Army Form C. 2118

Place	Date	Hour	Summary of Events and Information	Remarks and references to Appendices
RIMBOVAL	1/12/15		General routine. Rain.	
RIMBOVAL	2/12/15		General routine. Rain.	
RIMBOVAL	3/12/15		General routine. Rain.	
RIMBOVAL	4/12/15		General routine. Rain.	
RIMBOVAL	5/12/15		General routine. Rain.	
RIMBOVAL	6/12/15		Lieut. J. Hunt appointed temporarily to East Germany vice Capt. J. H. Benson accidentally wounded & evacuated to No 22 Casualty Clearing Station at Lillers. General routine. Rain.	
RIMBOVAL	7/12/15		Capt. R. M. WEDDERBURN one N.C.O. & nine men were relieved from duty in bomb at LYNDE. General routine. Rain.	
RIMBOVAL	8/12/15		Equipment of Field Ambulance checked & overhauled. General routine. Rain.	
RIMBOVAL	9/12/15		Surplus stores inspected by the D.A.D.R. of III Cav. Div. Two light draft horses evacuated to No 20 M.V.S. Major G. A. L. HAMMERTON, Staff Off. Health on leave, appointed to command No 6 Cavalry Field Ambulance. General routine. Rain.	
RIMBOVAL	10/12/15		Lieut. J. LUMB went to unite within billeting area of East Germany.	

Army Form C. 2118

WAR DIARY
or
INTELLIGENCE SUMMARY
(Erase heading not required.)

Instructions regarding War Diaries and Intelligence Summaries are contained in F. S. Regs., Part II. and the Staff Manual respectively. Title Pages will be prepared in manuscript.

Place	Date	Hour	Summary of Events and Information	Remarks and references to Appendices
RIMBOVAL	11/12/15		Five light draught horses + one riding horse evacuated to No 8 M.V.S. vide instructions D.A.D.R. III CAV DIV. General routine. Rain.	
RIMBOVAL	12/12/15		General routine. Rain.	
RIMBOVAL	13/12/15		Capt J. GROVE-WHITE returned from leave to England + reported for duty. R. J. LUMB proceeded to England on leave of absence. Capt J.H. BENSON returned from No 22 Casualty Clearing Station + reported for duty. General routine. Rain.	
RIMBOVAL	14/12/15		Capt J.H GROVE-WHITE took over charge of East Germany vice R.J LUMB. General routine. Rain.	
RIMBOVAL	15/12/15		General routine. Rain.	
RIMBOVAL	16/12/15		General routine. Rain.	
RIMBOVAL	17/12/15		Court martial assembled at RIMBOVAL for the trial of No 21 Corporal A.SELLORS R.A.M.C. + No.1175 Corporal T. DAVIES R.A.M.C. charged with (D) CORP. SELLORS — When on Active Service conduct to the prejudice of good order and military discipline in that he at RIMBOVAL on the night of the 4th December 1915:— (1) Created a disturbance in a billet where troops	

1875. Wt. W593/826. 1,000,000. 4/15. J.B.C.&A. A.D.S.S./Forms/C. 2118.

WAR DIARY or INTELLIGENCE SUMMARY

Army Form C. 2118

Place	Date	Hour	Summary of Events and Information	Remarks and references to Appendices
RIMBOVAL	17/12/15	Contd.	wear billets. He was acquitted. (2) Corporal DAVIES. When on Patrol Service, conduct to the prejudice of good order & military discipline in that he at RIMBOVAL on the night of the 4th December 1915:— (1) Sent up a disturbance in a house where men were billeted (2) Threatening to strike his superior officer No. 1161 Sgt. E. DRUMMOND RAME. (3) Striking an inhabitant of the country in which he was serving one FELIX MILLAURIAUX in that he at RIMBOVAL on the night of December the 4th 1915 Struck M. FELIX MILLAURIAUX footup (1) GUILTY (2) GUILTY Rau	
RIMBOVAL	18/12/15		General routine. Fine.	
RIMBOVAL	19/12/15		General routine. Rain.	
RIMBOVAL	20/12/15		Field Ambulance formed in full marching order for inspection by Officer Commanding 8th C.F.A. Arrangements made for establishing a Brigade bath at RIMBOVAL. Court martial on Corporals No.1175 ———— DAVIES R.A.M.C. (1) Guilty. (2) Not Guilty. (2) Guilty. Sentence — To be reduced to the ranks & to be imprisoned with hard labour for 84 days Commuted. to prison suspended under Suspension of Sentences Act. 1915. By F. O. C. 8th Cavalry Brigade. Approved	

Army Form C. 2118

WAR DIARY
or
INTELLIGENCE SUMMARY

(Erase heading not required.)

Instructions regarding War Diaries and Intelligence Summaries are contained in F.S. Regs., Part II. and the Staff Manual respectively. Title Pages will be prepared in manuscript.

Place	Date	Hour	Summary of Events and Information	Remarks and references to Appendices
RIMBOVAL	21/12/15		Inspection of Field Ambulance by the A.D.M.S. III Cav. Div. General routine. Rain.	
RIMBOVAL	22/12/15		No 1099 Sgt. A. COOK reverted to the rank of driver at his own request. No 1138. Farrier Corporal J. HOLBROOK promoted to the rank of Sergeant vice Sgt. COOK. General routine. Rain.	
RIMBOVAL	23/12/15		General routine. Rain.	
RIMBOVAL	24/12/15		General routine. New Napier motor ambulance arrived from H.Q. to replace Sunbeam. Rain	
RIMBOVAL	25/12/15		General routine. Rain.	
RIMBOVAL	26/12/15		General routine. Rain.	
RIMBOVAL	27/12/15		Order received from H.Q. III Cav Div. for personnel & equipment of No 12 (Corps) Cav Field Ambulance to hold itself in readiness for mobilization at short notice. General routine. Rain.	
RIMBOVAL	28/12/15		Parade for Inspection of O/C 8th C.F.A. of personnel of No 12 (Corps) Cav Field Ambulance. Rain.	
RIMBOVAL	29/12/15		General routine. Rain.	

WAR DIARY
or
INTELLIGENCE SUMMARY

Army Form C. 2118

Place	Date	Hour	Summary of Events and Information	Remarks and references to Appendices
RIMBOVAL	30/12/15		Received orders from A.D.M.S. III Cav Div for motor ambulance details for the 3rd Cav Div Comp Field Ambulance to report at A.D.M.S. office Rimboval noon on 1st prox. also for the detachment of NCO & men detailed for the 3rd Cav Div Comp Field Ambulance to be under two hours notice after twelve noon on the 31st inst. General routine. Kept.	
RIMBOVAL	3/1/16		Received orders from A.D.M.S. 3rd Cav Div for the detachment details for the 3rd Cav Div Field Ambulance to leave RIMBOVAL as coln. for the 3rd Cav Div Comp Field Ambulance to proceed to MARESQUEL reporting to them 8.30 a.m. on the 19th inst. & to proceed to MARESQUEL reporting to arrival to Major G.H.L. HAMMERTON before 2.30 P.M.	
		8.30 p.m.	Received orders from A.D.M.S. 3rd Cav Div for the motor ambulance two given - two details - leaves to report forthwith to the A.D.M.S. 3rd Cav Div MD proceed for duty with the 3rd Cav Div Comp Field Ambulance. General routine. Rain.	

3-1-16

[signature]
Lieut. Col. R.A.M.C.
O.C. 8th C.F.A.

8 Cav 7d Amb
Vol XIV

Army Form C. 2118

WAR DIARY or INTELLIGENCE SUMMARY

(Erase heading not required.)

Instructions regarding War Diaries and Intelligence Summaries are contained in F.S. Regs., Part II. and the Staff Manual respectively. Title Pages will be prepared in manuscript.

Place	Date	Hour	Summary of Events and Information	Remarks and references to Appendices
RIMBOVAL	1/1/16	8 A.M.	One Officer, 28 N.C.O.s & men departed on detachment to the III Cav Div Field Ambulance proceeding to MARESQUEL together with 1 two horse light ambulance wagon, one G.S. wagon & one water cart. Four additional drivers (horse) were sent for duty with the III Cav Div (Cav) Field Ambulance. Rain.	
RIMBOVAL	2/1/16		Two squadrons of the Royal Horse Guards were billeted so many G.S. wagons of No 8 Cavalry Field Ambulance at the horse lines at RIMBOVAL. Proper motor ambulance No A15983 damaged in collision with incoming G.S. wagon at BETHUNE. Rain.	
RIMBOVAL	3/1/16		General Routine. Rain.	
RIMBOVAL	4/1/16		General Routine. Rain.	
RIMBOVAL	5/1/16		General Routine. Rain.	
RIMBOVAL	6/1/16		General Routine. Rain.	
RIMBOVAL	7/1/16		Motor ambulance No A17854 sent to III Cav Div F.A.W.U. for overhaul & repair. Motor ambulance No A9995 reported for duty from H.Q. III Cav Div.	

General Routine. R.C. &.A.

Army Form C. 2118

WAR DIARY
or
INTELLIGENCE SUMMARY
(Erase heading not required.)

Instructions regarding War Diaries and Intelligence Summaries are contained in F.S. Regs., Part II. and the Staff Manual respectively. Title Pages will be prepared in manuscript.

Place	Date	Hour	Summary of Events and Information	Remarks and references to Appendices
RIMBOVAL	8/1/16		General Routine. Rain.	
RIMBOVAL	9/1/16		General Routine. Rain.	
RIMBOVAL	10/1/16		General Routine. Rain.	
RIMBOVAL	11/1/16		General Routine. Capt. A.H. BENSON R.A.M.C. on leave to England. Rain.	
RIMBOVAL	12/1/16		General Routine. Rain.	
RIMBOVAL	13/1/16		General Routine. Rain.	
RIMBOVAL	14/1/16		140th Ambulance No 217854 returns to duty from F.A.W.V. 1st Cav Div	
RIMBOVAL	15/1/16		General Routine. Rain.	
RIMBOVAL	16/1/16		General Routine. Rain.	
RIMBOVAL	17/1/16		General Routine. Trotter Ambulance No 9995 ordered to report to No 6 C.C.S. S. ADMS to Cav S.in for duty. Rain.	
RIMBOVAL	18/1/16		Capt. E.M. WEDDERBURN took over medical charge of IX Royal Hussars vice Capt. S.H. CLARKE proceeding for duty with 8th Batt Devonshire Cav. General Routine. Rain.	

1875 Wt. W593/826 1,000,000 4/15 J.B.C. & A. A.D.S.S./Forms/C. 2118.

Army Form C. 2118

WAR DIARY
or
INTELLIGENCE SUMMARY

(Erase heading not required.)

Instructions regarding War Diaries and Intelligence Summaries are contained in F. S. Regs., Part II. and the Staff Manual respectively. Title Pages will be prepared in manuscript.

Place	Date	Hour	Summary of Events and Information	Remarks and references to Appendices
RIMBOVAL	19/1/16		General routine. Rain	
RIMBOVAL	20/1/16		General routine. Rain.	
RIMBOVAL	21/1/16		General routine. Rain.	
RIMBOVAL	22/1/16		General routine. Rain.	
RIMBOVAL	23/1/16		General routine. Rain.	
RIMBOVAL	24/1/16		General routine. Rain.	
RIMBOVAL	25/1/16		General routine. Rain.	
RIMBOVAL	26/1/16		General routine. A.D.M.S. III Corps D.is visited inspected transport & bathing arrangements. Rain.	
RIMBOVAL	27/1/16		Lt. Col. W. KITSON CLAYTON to England on seven days leave of absence. General routine. Rain.	
RIMBOVAL	28/1/16		A.D.M.S. visited 8th C.F.A. General routine. Rain.	
RIMBOVAL	29/1/16		General routine. Rain.	

1875 Wt. W503/826 1,000,000 4/15 I.B.C. & A. A.D.S.S./Forms/C. 2118.

Army Form C. 2118

WAR DIARY
or
INTELLIGENCE SUMMARY

(Erase heading not required.)

Instructions regarding War Diaries and Intelligence Summaries are contained in F. S. Regs., Part II. and the Staff Manual respectively. Title Pages will be prepared in manuscript.

Place	Date	Hour	Summary of Events and Information	Remarks and references to Appendices
RIMBOVAL	30/1/16		General Nature A&O	
"	31/1/16		Eight ambulance waggons drawn to the R.A.M.C. orderly stationed at Floringhem. Issued day's ration of Royal Field Service Reserve ration to A&HB.	

Wellington
Lieut Colonel R.A.M.C.
D.D. 8th C.F.A.

WAR DIARY or INTELLIGENCE SUMMARY

Army Form C. 2118

Place	Date	Hour	Summary of Events and Information	Remarks and references to Appendices
QIMBOVAL	1.2.16		Leivere Routine. a.o.b.	
"	2.2.16		Leivere Routine a.o.b.	
"	3.2.16		Lieut Col W.R. Clayton returned from leave in England. Leivere Routine a.o.b	
"	4.2.16		The R.A.M.C. reinforcements returned to duty. Leivere Routine a.o.b.	
"	5.2.16		Leivere Routine a.o.b.	
"	6.2.16		Leivere Routine a.o.b.	
"	7.2.16		Capt A.F. Jordan MRCS on leave to England. Leivere Routine a.o.b.	
"	8.2.16		Leivere Routine a.o.b.	
"	9.2.16		Leivere Routine a.o.b	
"	10.2.16		Leivere Routine a.o.b	
"	11.2.16		Leivere Routine a.o.b	
"	12.2.16		Lt Col Duff and two Lieuts A.C.O.s and 2 O.R.i with equipment returned from leave a.o.b. Field Ambulance. Two Lieuts relieved R.M.C. killed	
"	13.2.16		Leivere Routine a.o.b.	
"	14.2.16		Leivere Routine a.o.b.	
"	15.2.16		Leivere Routine a.o.b	
"	16.2.16		Leivere Routine a.o.b	
"	17.2.16		Lieut R.P. Slaughty RAMC returned on duty. Leivere Routine a.o.b	
"	18.2.16		Leivere Routine a.o.b	
"	19.2.16		Leivere Routine a.o.b	
"	20.2.16		Capt LAMORAN returned from leave in England. Leivere Routine a.o.b	
"	21.2.16		Lieut W.K. CLAYTON left on leave for England. Leivere Routine a.o.b	
"	22.2.16		Lieut D.F. DOBSON RAMC (78) took over medical charge. Leivere Routine a.o.b	
"	23.2.16		Col R. MARSHALL RAMC M.O. to leave to England. Leivere Routine a.o.b	
"	24.2.16		Leivere Routine a.o.b	
"	25.2.16		Returned over 10th R HUSSARS killed. Leivere Routine a.o.b	
"	26.2.16		Die two two over 10th R HUSSARS killed. Leivere Routine a.o.b	
"	27.2.16		Leivere Routine a.o.b	

Army Form C. 2118

WAR DIARY
or
INTELLIGENCE SUMMARY
(Erase heading not required.)

Instructions regarding War Diaries and Intelligence Summaries are contained in F. S. Regs., Part II. and the Staff Manual respectively. Title Pages will be prepared in manuscript.

Place	Date	Hour	Summary of Events and Information	Remarks and references to Appendices
RIMBOVAL	28.2/16		Lieut Col W.R. CLAYTON returns from leave in England. Service routine carried out	
"	29.2/16		Service routine carried out. During the have month a considerable amount of excellent work has been done in the trenches. Several cases of influenza and an epidemic of measles and mumps in the Essex Regiment. ASC	

Walter Clayton
Lieut Colonel RAMC
O.C. 8th F.A.

8th Cav. Field Ambulance

Jan
Feb } 1916
Mar

3 C

8 Cav 1d Amb
Vol XV

WAR DIARY or INTELLIGENCE SUMMARY

Army Form C. 2118

Place	Date	Hour	Summary of Events and Information	Remarks and references to Appendices
RIMBOVAL	1.3.16		Received orders from N O's 8th Cav Brigade that the 8th Cav Bde when exchange billets with was to with 16' Cav Div, and are enrolled by 6 PM on March 3rd 1916. General Routine AoHB	
"	2.3.16		General Routine AoHB	
"	3.3.16		Equipment, harness & havelocks wagons and bell room dis-mantled. General Routine AoHB	
"	3.3.16	9 PM	order for move came. ell'd AoHB	
"	4.3.16		Unhorsed squad moved from riggers to General Routine AoHB	
"	5.3.16		2.00 a.m. 10th R. HUSSARS halted. A 1109 No to ambulance 11.45 a.m into feed ambulance and 9th R. Haus. Lancashire Ambulance AoHB	
"	6.3.16		2.00 a.m. 10th R HUSSARS halted. A 1115 Rosin ambulance arrived in duty. General Routine AoHB	
"	7.3.16		General Routine. Snow Storm. AoHB	
"	8.3.16		General Routine Occup (5 dies free of Snow were to advance 16 hours & horses were requned for lying ambulances. Awake returns put during day AoHB	
"	9.3.16		General Routine Weather tried hot cold two orderly privates attached for duty with weekly forward Brigade Headrne Sun Squadron Motor ambulance AoHB	
"	10.3.16		General routine Ambulance 1/69 returns from Marshka ambulance 11/15 Sent to workshop for 24 hours received. Lieut A of AB	

Army Form C. 2118

WAR DIARY
or
INTELLIGENCE SUMMARY
(Erase heading not required.)

Instructions regarding War Diaries and Intelligence Summaries are contained in F. S. Regs., Part II. and the Staff Manual respectively. Title Pages will be prepared in manuscript.

Place	Date	Hour	Summary of Events and Information	Remarks and references to Appendices
RIMBOVAL	11/3/16		General routine. Water Cart (Hicks) sent to A.O. workshop. I/M Carley sent to Hosps.	
"	12/3/16		Another as unusual. Obtained milk, RH6s at Auga Ossai changed. Reported to duty. Weather fine and warmer — 30°F.	
"	13/3/16		Received telegram A. Druss. 3 Cow Sr. notifying Capt A.H. BENSON to proceed to ENGLAND to take over command of 3rd Line unit. General Routine. Weather fine. Thunderstorm 6 p.m. (A.)	
"	14/3/16		Capt A.H. BENSON proceeded to ENGLAND. Notification received of infection of unit by A. Drus. 3rd Cow Div on 16 inst at 11 a.m. 200 N. Costumes distributed. Today Weather fine & warm (A.)	
"	15/3/16		Inspection Parade in full marching order with arms & equipment. Strength on Parade 5 Offrs 80 other ranks by G.O. Lecture on 1st Aid by Capt Hobbs. 193 river of 5 Res. horses attended bathing parade weather fine (A).	
"	16/3/16		The 16 Ambulance was inspected by the W. Drus. Parade strength 60 ffs 88 other ranks. 46 horses 6 ambulance wagons 2 G.S. 2 Lunches waggons 1 forage cart 1 water Cart. The G.O.C. 6th Cavalry Brigade decorated Corporal H. Corley 1147 with the Russian medal of St. George for distinguished conduct in the field on 14/9/15. Weather fine (A).	

WAR DIARY
or
INTELLIGENCE SUMMARY.

(Erase heading not required.)

Army Form C. 2118.

Hour, Date, Place	Summary of Events and Information	Remarks and references to Appendices
RIMBOVAL 17.3.16	Parade Physical drill. 1 Staff Sergt. Next proceeded to Scores Junction for stretcher drill training & to Gwent to this unit by three leather pine S/s	
" 18.3.16	3t Ambulance received in Physical Company and Stretcher drill. Capt J Bowie D.S.O. reports for duty. (Leather pine S/s)	
" 19.3.16	C of parade in marching order 2 inspection of Clothing & Equipment. All knapsacks, belts & clasps were inspected and found in good order. One Motor driver found to be suffering from scabies. Was evacuated to Div Sans Hosp & contacts indiv + billet disinfected. (Leaves out of "Bruds" Leather pine S/s)	

Army Form C. 2118.

WAR DIARY
or
INTELLIGENCE SUMMARY.

(Erase heading not required.)

Instructions regarding War Diaries and Intelligence Summaries are contained in F.S. Regs., Part II. and the Staff Manual respectively. Title pages will be prepared in manuscript.

Hour, Date, Place	Summary of Events and Information	Remarks and references to Appendices
Hutefield March 20. 1916 RIMBOVAL	Recruits exercised in Company drill, Horses of billets scrubbed. In addition which the the horses clothes was disinfected again. Weather overcast. S.A.	
" March 21. 1916	Completed the painting of light ambulance cars. Purchased 2 barrels for was tub for following purposes. No 120 8½ lbs substitutes for duty with R.N.V. in place of No 1166 Pte Heard & No Sucks. 150 rolls of X Ray paper notted S.A.	
	Lt. of 8th C.Y.A. weather wet. S.A.	
" March 22nd 1916	Major DOBSON proceeded on leave to ENGLAND. Bottle bath received from Ordnance to replace one broken. Rec'd the 20 boxes of X.R. Nervous Batteries Battn Obstarct. M. medical Capt. J. LUMB both over charge temporarily of R.N.V. vice Surg Major P.M. COWIE. C.O. inspected all equipment lubs or charge weather wet. S.A.	
" 23"		

Army Form C. 2118.

WAR DIARY
or
INTELLIGENCE SUMMARY.
(Erase heading not required.)

Instructions regarding War Diaries and Intelligence Summaries are contained in F. S. Regs., Part II. and the Staff Manual respectively. Title pages will be prepared in manuscript.

Hour, Date, Place	Summary of Events and Information	Remarks and references to Appendices
RIMBOVAL March 24th 1916	Orderly room with changes to another line. Case of measles reported in village. General routine. 8 pr. present generally washes and baths. Weather cold, dull and wet. (A)	
RIMBOVAL Mar 25/1916	General Routine, Rain 8 o'c 2)	
RIMBOVAL Mar 26/1916	Two R.A.M.C. reinforcements to rescue. Wet & windy 2)	
RIMBOVAL Mar 27/1916	Genl. x0 Routine, Company Drill. Fine 9 o'c 6 2)	
RIMBOVAL Mar 28/1916	General routine. Ambulance A/1096 w20726SD 180 men 10R knees baths. Wet 2 0	

Army Form C. 2118.

WAR DIARY
or
INTELLIGENCE SUMMARY.
(Erase heading not required.)

Instructions regarding War Diaries and Intelligence Summaries are contained in F. S. Regs., Part II. and the Staff Manual respectively. Title pages will be prepared in manuscript.

Place	Date	Hour	Summary of Events and Information	Remarks and references to Appendices
RIMBOVAL	29/3/16		Service Routine. One water cart received. The Numbers 10th R. Hussars lectures. Lieut. Col. 2nd	
RIMBOVAL	30/3/16		Transport inspected by O.C. A.S.C. 111 Cav. Div. Lent one Lecture by visiting officers. Two dummy Rd	
RIMBOVAL	31/3/16		Reveille 5.30 17 men E. and C. Routine. Two dummy.	

W. H. Anderton Lt Col. R.A.M.C.
O.C. 8th Cav. Fld. Amb.

War Diary

of

No. 8. Cav. Field Ambulance

for

April 1916.

3C

8 Cav Fd Amb

Vol. XVI

COMMITTEE FOR THE
MEDICAL HISTORY OF THE WAR
Date   9 - JUN 1916

WAR DIARY
or
INTELLIGENCE SUMMARY.
(Erase heading not required.)

Army Form C. 2118.

Instructions regarding War Diaries and Intelligence Summaries are contained in F. S. Regs. Part II. and the Staff Manual respectively. Title pages will be prepared in manuscript.

Place	Date	Hour	Summary of Events and Information	Remarks and references to Appendices
RIMBOVAL	1/4/16		One L.D. horse evacuated to 26th mobile vet section. Cap't LUMB reported from R.H.S. for duty. Fine & hot	2D
RIMBOVAL	2/4/16		Cap't HOBBS on leave to ENGLAND. Cap't J LUMB to 4th R.B.S. M.H.A. for duty. Fine & hot.	2D
RIMBOVAL	3/4/16		Eighth man medical Inn Sgt 10th R. Hussars rifles. General routine. Weather hot.	2D
RIMBOVAL	4/4/16		Bath for X Royal Hussars — 178 men. Fine & hot	2D
RIMBOVAL	5/4/16		Bath for X Royal Hussars 170 men. Weather fine	2D
RIMBOVAL	6/4/16		Company mule A1189 wolog cav. sent to FARM 3rd Cav. Div. Horses inspected by ADVS. Weather fine & cool	2D

Army Form C. 2118.

WAR DIARY
or
INTELLIGENCE SUMMARY.
(Erase heading not required.)

Instructions regarding War Diaries and Intelligence Summaries are contained in F. S. Regs., Part II. and the Staff Manual respectively. Title pages will be prepared in manuscript.

Place	Date	Hour	Summary of Events and Information	Remarks and references to Appendices
RIMBOVAL	7/10		Route march. 2 men R.A.M.C. Sunbeam Car 1115 reported for duty. Weather fine	
RIMBOVAL	8/10		Wash Cart returned to ordnance. Runner Rodine went to join 2D. Weather fine	
RIMBOVAL	9/10		Practice drill. All equipment packed ready in full marching order. Weather fine	
RIMBOIRAL	10/10		A.M.D.S. to F.A.W.M. for rehearsal also his light ambulances. A.D.S. reported for ors from F.A.W.M. General Rodine. Weather fine	
RIMBOVAL	11/10		General Rodine. Wet. Pte MAGEE 77379 to rest - Emergt line Cambs for exchange	

2353 Wt W2541/1454 700,000 5/15 D. D. & L. A.D.S.S./Forms/C. 2118.

WAR DIARY
or
INTELLIGENCE SUMMARY.
(Erase heading not required.)

Army Form C. 2118.

Place	Date	Hour	Summary of Events and Information	Remarks and references to Appendices
RIMBOVAL	12/6/16		Horse & Raid set the funnessan Eneral Routine 185 men 10 R Munsters baths, also 10 R.A.M.C Very wet	
RIMBOVAL	13/6/16		195 men 10 R Munsters baths. One E.S. wagon to III field Guns for repair. Routine Dull, showery	
RIMBOVAL	14/6/16		Routine work. Capt. SLANEY returns from leave. Dull showery	
RIMBOVAL	15/6/16		Eneral routine. weather fine	
RIMBOVAL	16/6/16		A.D.M.S. III Cav Div inspects transport ready for march. Telegram memo from O.C. no II London Gen Hospital that Capt. HOBBS travels 2 nd week leave. I/c no 1 permanents unfit for normal duty. Weath fine	

WAR DIARY
or
INTELLIGENCE SUMMARY.

(Erase heading not required.)

Army Form C. 2118

Place	Date	Hour	Summary of Events and Information	Remarks and references to Appendices
RIMBOVAL	17/6		One light ambulance to F.A.W.U. for repairs also one he horses from F.A.W.U. Weather wet & cold	20
RIMBOVAL	18/6		General Routine. One light ambulance from F.A.W.U. & one sent in for repairs. Wet & cold	20
RIMBOVAL	19/6		183 men 10 O.R. Horses halted the night and from F.A.W.U. & one return to Indian Cav Depot Pickardt. returned from leave. Weather wet	20
RIMBOVAL	20/6		166 men 16 R.Horses (+2 O.) 30 R.A.M.C. also Two light ambulances returned from F.A.W.U. Weather wet	20
RIMBOVAL	21/6		General Routine. One Y.M.B.F.A. driver recruit arrived from M.I. Cavalry Base Depot Rouen. Weather wet & cold	20

WAR DIARY
or
INTELLIGENCE SUMMARY.
(Erase heading not required.)

Army Form C. 2118.

Instructions regarding War Diaries and Intelligence Summaries are contained in F. S. Regs., Part II. and the Staff Manual respectively. Title pages will be prepared in manuscript.

Place	Date	Hour	Summary of Events and Information	Remarks and references to Appendices
RIMBOVAL	22/4/16		General Routine Lt H PRINGLE R.A.M.C. to act for No 24 General Hospital vice J.C.C. 2 D	
RIMBOVAL	23/4/16		Inspection of Personnel of unit by D.R. Stone 2 D	
RIMBOVAL	24/4/16		Two Officers and 28 men joined D.R.S. for and from Germany 2 D	
RIMBOVAL	25/4/16		Interchanged 10 R Hussars Halks & 23 R.A.M.C Capt LUHB (on duty to R.H.G.) Weather Wet 2 D	
RIMBOVAL	26/4/16		165 10 R Hussars Halks & 20 R.A.M.C Three A.S.C. Reinforcement reports for duty. Two I D Horses from 13th Mob Vet Section Weather Wet 2 D	

Army Form C. 2118.

WAR DIARY
or
INTELLIGENCE SUMMARY.
(Erase heading not required.)

Instructions regarding War Diaries and Intelligence Summaries are contained in F. S. Regs., Part II. and the Staff Manual respectively. Title pages will be prepared in manuscript.

Place	Date	Hour	Summary of Events and Information	Remarks and references to Appendices
RIMBOVAL	27/10		One rider gone to D. Note from Lieut. Capt. MORAN on leave to ENGLAND. Weather N.S. 2⁰	
RIMBOVAL	28/10		General Routine. One R.A.M.C. reinforcement from Base. Weather N.S. 2⁰	
RIMBOVAL	29/10		General Routine. One Riding Horse from 20th Inf. Bde. section. Weather N.S. 2⁰	
RIMBOVAL	30/10		Inspection of unit by C.O. General Routine. Weather N.S. 2⁰	

Milton Ampton
Lieut. Col. R.A.M.C.
O.C. 8th Cav. Fd. Amb.

May 1st

3rd Can Div

8th Can. I.A.

D.A.G.
3rd Echelon,
Base

[stamp: No 8 CAVALRY FIELD AMBULANCE
A.D.56
5.6.16]

Herewith War Diary
for this unit for the month
of May, 1916

[signature]
Lt. Col. R.A.M.C.
5/6/16   O.C. No 8 Cav. Fd. Amb.

WAR DIARY or INTELLIGENCE SUMMARY
Army Form C. 2118.

Vol 19

Place	Date	Hour	Summary of Events and Information	Remarks and references to Appendices
RIMBOVAL	1 5/6		The light Amb. will down to R.H.Q. for duty while on manœuvres. Weather hot. 2D	
RIMBOVAL	2 5/6		General Routine – 185 men 10 R Hussars & 35. R.A.M.C bathed – Warm Showery 2D	
RIMBOVAL	3 5/6		185 men 10 R Hussars & 30 R.A.M.C men bathed – H.S.T. 2D	
RIMBOVAL	4 5/6		General Routine – H.S.T. 2D	
RIMBOVAL	5 5/6		General Routine 1st R.A.M.C reinforcement rec'd H.S.T. 2D	
RIMBOVAL	6 5/6		General Routine CAPT MORAN returns from leave CAPT LUNB departs on leave to ENGLAND Warm 2D	

WAR DIARY
or
INTELLIGENCE SUMMARY.

Army Form C. 2118.

Place	Date	Hour	Summary of Events and Information	Remarks and references to Appendices
RIMBOVAL	8/5/16		General Routine. CAPT MORAN & two OR sick to Ambulance. 10/5/16 Left for Conference held with 82 Machine Gun Squad	2D
RIMBOVAL	9/5/16		General Routine — wet	2D
RIMBOVAL	9/5/16		186 and 10th R.H. warm baths & 20 RAMC 2R rising & overs received from Rail — wet	2D
RIMBOVAL	10/5/16		186 & R.H. warm baths & 10 RAMC — warm	2D
RIMBOVAL	11/5/16		General Routine — warm	2D
RIMBOVAL	12/5/16		General Routine — warm	2D
RIMBOVAL	13/5/16		General Routine. CAPT LUMB from leave returning	2D

WAR DIARY
or
INTELLIGENCE SUMMARY.

Army Form C. 2118.

Place	Date	Hour	Summary of Events and Information	Remarks and references to Appendices
Quévord	14/5/16		General Routine. Capt Sluney & Lt Pringle returned from temporary duty at D.R.S. Capt Moran & there O.R. & L.A. Wagon (Reserves) from temporary duty with No 8 W S. Capt Moran proceeded for temporary duty at D.R.S. Weather dull.	O.R.S.
Puyelle en Chaussé	16/5/16		Lt-Col. W. J. Clayton Capt Sluney & Lt Pringle & 34 O.R. 21 Horses & 2 G.S. wagons 2 Lim. water carts and proceeded with 8th Cav Bde to taking over billets at NOYELLE-E-11-CHAUSSÉE. Lt Pringle took over tented and reserved 2 Sanitary change of 8. Batt R.H.A Walker Wet till 6 P.M. Overnight fine. General Routine. Hospital established at the Mairie for the 15 to 20 men of A. Wagon returned from duty with G. H. G.S. Weather fine	O.R.S. O.R.S. O.R.S.
NOYELLE-E-H-CHAUSSÉE	17/5/16		General Routine. Weather fine.	O.R.S.

Army Form C. 2118.

WAR DIARY
or
INTELLIGENCE SUMMARY.
(Erase heading not required.)

Instructions regarding War Diaries and Intelligence Summaries are contained in F.S. Regs., Part II. and the Staff Manual respectively. Title pages will be prepared in manuscript.

Place	Date	Hour	Summary of Events and Information	Remarks and references to Appendices
MOYELLE EN CHAUSSEE	18/5/16		Lt. Col. Clayton Capt Dally + detachment moved off at 6 A.M. to Brigade sports — who at YVRENCH + returned to billets at 5 P.M. Weather fine	R S
MOYELLE EN CHAUSSEE	19/5/16		General Routine Weather fine	R S
MOYELLE EN CHAUSSEE	20/5/16		Lt. Col. Clayton left at 6-30 A.M. for manoeuvres with the Brigadier General & his Bde. Bdg. Returned at 3-30 P.M. Weather fine & warm	R S
MOYELLE EN CHAUSSEE	21/5/16		The Ambulance returned to Rumboval from manoeuvre area at 5-30 A.M. arriving Rumboval at 1 P.M. Weather fine & warm	R S
RUMBOVAL	22/5/16		General Routine Weather fine & warm	R S

2353 Wt W2544/1454 700,000 5/15 D.D.&L. A.D.S.S./Forms/C.2118.

Army Form C. 2118.

WAR DIARY
or
INTELLIGENCE SUMMARY.
(Erase heading not required.)

Instructions regarding War Diaries and Intelligence Summaries are contained in F. S. Regs., Part II. and the Staff Manual respectively. Title pages will be prepared in manuscript.

Place	Date	Hour	Summary of Events and Information	Remarks and references to Appendices
RIMBOVAL	23/5/16		2.00 am 10th R.H. entered General routine weather fine winds	R S
RIMBOVAL	24/5/16		General routine. Lt Cringle left this day on seven days leave 15 Ireland weather fine	R S
RIMBOVAL	25/5/16		General routine Weather fine	R S
RIMBOVAL	26/5/16		General routine Weather fine	R S
RIMBOVAL	27/5/16		General routine Weather fine	R S
RIMBOVAL	28/5/16		General routine Capt J Dowrie D.S.C proceed on 14 days leave to Scotland Weather fine	R S

Army Form C. 2118.

WAR DIARY
or
INTELLIGENCE SUMMARY.
(Erase heading not required.)

Place	Date	Hour	Summary of Events and Information	Remarks and references to Appendices
RUMBOVAL	29/5/16		Mounted advance party completed equipment & horse lines who inspected by the A.D.M.S. 3rd Cav. Div. Details for detail breakdown 4th & 8th Cav. Brigades are as under: To 6 Convalescent Depot Etaples. Received order from Brig. Hq. to move to MERLIMONT on 31st inst. Weather fine RS	
RUMBOVAL	30/5/16		One by 4 ambulance wagon returned from detached duty with the Royal Horse Guards. All men of the Field ambulance [billeted?] Weather fine. Billeting Officers proceeded to MERLIMONT to arrange billets RS	
RUMBOVAL	31/5/16		32nd Field Ambulance left RUMBOVAL at 8-30 A.M. and proceeded via BAURAINVILLE arriving at MERLIMONT at 4-30 P.M. & occupied bivouacs. Weather fine RS	

Ph.W. Clayton
Lieut. Colonel R.A.M.C.
O.C. 8th Cav. Fld. Amb.

2nd Cav Divn ?

9th Cavalry Field Ambulance

June 1916

Army Form C. 2118.

WAR DIARY
or
INTELLIGENCE SUMMARY.
(Erase heading not required.)

Vol 14 + 18

Place	Date	Hour	Summary of Events and Information	Remarks and references to Appendices
MERLIMONT	1/6/16		Detail on hospital opened for treatment of troops of 3rd Cav DW. occupying this area. One L.A. wagon returned from detached duty with 10th R Sy. One Officer & 29 other ranks returned from duty at D.R.S. FRUGES. A.Gringle returned from leave to IRLAND. Walker June & week.	
MERLIMONT	2/6/16		Rev. bathing parade for all ranks & transport horses. Walks June & week.	Q.S.
MERLIMONT	3/6/16		Sea bathing men & horses. General routine. True	
MERLIMONT	4/6/16		The T.O. horse dies. General routine, nothing true	
MERLIMONT	5/6/16		Fifteen venereal cases to hospital. General routine, bathing etc.	ED

Army Form C. 2118.

WAR DIARY
or
INTELLIGENCE SUMMARY.
(Erase heading not required.)

Instructions regarding War Diaries and Intelligence Summaries are contained in F. S. Regs., Part II. and the Staff Manual respectively. Title pages will be prepared in manuscript.

Place	Date	Hour	Summary of Events and Information	Remarks and references to Appendices
MERLIMONT	6/6/16		Our finding horse 216 – Another leg – Ice bathing – Fine Hot	2D
MERLIMONT	7/6/16		Received orders for awarding vacancies in Bony destined on 14, 15, 16, 17 inst – General routine Fine	2D
MERLIMONT	8/6/16		General routine Capt DOWNIE returned from Leave Fine	2D
MERLIMONT	9/6/16		CAPT LUMB J took over medical charge R.M.S. vice SURG MAJOR COWIE on leave to ENGLAND General Routine Rain	2D
MERLIMONT	10/6/16		Red ulcers returned to permanent billets RIMBOVAL Fine Hot	2D
RIMBOVAL	11/6/16		General Routine Fine	2D

Army Form C. 2118.

WAR DIARY
or
INTELLIGENCE SUMMARY.
(Erase heading not required.)

Instructions regarding War Diaries and Intelligence Summaries are contained in F. S. Regs., Part II. and the Staff Manual respectively. Title pages will be prepared in manuscript.

Place	Date	Hour	Summary of Events and Information	Remarks and references to Appendices
RIMBOVAL	14/4/16		Inspection of A Echelon by O.C. Marwoeuvres for 14 & 15th army cancelled Capt L.A. MORAN for duty to 1st Royal Dragoons Lt Col CLAYTON WK on leave to ENGLAND C.O. sick	
RIMBOVAL	15/4/16		General Picture Cold & wet	
RIMBOVAL	16/4/16		Horses picked out, 16 draught horses received & riding horse returned from 20th M.V.S. Cold	
RIMBOVAL	17/4/16		General Routine Claims Officer under took ?	
RIMBOVAL	18/4/16		Lecture by riding Officer on transfusion 3 weeks RAMC Details attached leg wound to Turner Lun b cann A1115.9 Dray ton reston cycle to hospital fine	

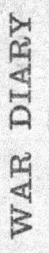

2353 Wt. W2544/1454 700,000 5/15 D.D.&L. A.D.S.S./Forms/C. 2118.

Army Form C. 2118.

WAR DIARY
or
INTELLIGENCE SUMMARY.
(Erase heading not required.)

Place	Date	Hour	Summary of Events and Information	Remarks and references to Appendices
RUMBOVAL	17/4/16		CAPT L A MORAN returned from temporary duty with 1st R. Dragoons. General Routine.	
RUMBOVAL	18/4/16		Clothing inspection. also P.H hole Returns, harness & saddlery. General Routine.	
RUMBOVAL	19/4/16		350 men 10 R Hussars Lathes. General Routine.	
RUMBOVAL	20/4/16		Lecture to N.C.O.s & men by order of Officers. Foot & leg care (in cov'd)	
RUMBOVAL	21/4/16		Lecture by order Officer on gas Precautions, Fuse	
RUMBOVAL	22/4/16		Lecture on water for [reaction?] Fire	

Army Form C. 2118.

WAR DIARY
or
INTELLIGENCE SUMMARY.
(Erase heading not required.)

Instructions regarding War Diaries and Intelligence Summaries are contained in F. S. Regs., Part II. and the Staff Manual respectively. Title pages will be prepared in manuscript.

Place	Date	Hour	Summary of Events and Information	Remarks and references to Appendices
RIMBOVAL	28/6/16		Packing equipment. Parade Inspector of water bottles & water bottles.	
RIMBOVAL	29/6/16		By Brigade orders left RIMBOVAL 2-30 P.M. Weather fine	
REGNIERE ECLUSE	29/6/16		Arrived REGNIERE ECLUSE 3 A.M. Orders to be in marching order at 8 August starting point 8 P.M. Capt. LUMB reported for duty. Weather fine	
ST OUEN	26/6/16		Arrived ST OUEN 3 A.M. Marching order starting point 8 P.M. Weather wet	
BONNAY	27/6/16		Arrived BONNAY 3-15 A.M. Wet	

Army Form C. 2118.

WAR DIARY
or
INTELLIGENCE SUMMARY.
(Erase heading not required.)

Instructions regarding War Diaries and Intelligence Summaries are contained in F. S. Regs., Part II. and the Staff Manual respectively. Title pages will be prepared in manuscript.

Place	Date	Hour	Summary of Events and Information	Remarks and references to Appendices
BONNAY	28/4/16		Staying by W.L	
BONNAY	29/4/16		Staying by W.L	
BONNAY	30/4/16		Staying by. Inspection of A1 Echelon by C.O.	
			by Line CD	

8-7-16

[signature]
OC 8° Cavalry Field Ambulance

Vol 19

3rd Cav Div.
No. 8 Cav Fld. Amb.

War diary of
Officer Jn. charge
of July 1916

M Bennett
Lieut. Col. R.A.M.C.
A.D.M.S. 3rd Cav. Div.

COMMITTEE FOR THE
MEDICAL HISTORY OF THE WAR
Date 13 SEP. 1915

July.

Army Form C. 2118.

WAR DIARY
or
INTELLIGENCE SUMMARY.
(Erase heading not required.)

Place	Date	Hour	Summary of Events and Information	Remarks and references to Appendices
BONNAY	1/4/16		Standing by	
BONNAY	2/4/16		Standing by 2 hrs notice. Cap.tn MORAN to Motor and convoy Hot. 2D	
BONNAY	3/4/16		Standing by 4 hrs notice Cap.tn MORAN returned for all Received orders to prepare to move to ABBEVILLE area on 4th inst. 2D	
BONNAY	4/4/16		Left at 5 AM arrived BAILLEUL 5 PM tine 2D	
BAILLEUL	5/4/16		Ennead Routine Line 2D	
BAILLEUL	6/4/16		Ennead Routine Line 2D	
BAILLEUL	7/4/16		Standing by 1 hrs notice from 6AM Wed 2D	

Army Form C. 2118.

WAR DIARY
or
INTELLIGENCE SUMMARY.

(Erase heading not required.)

Instructions regarding War Diaries and Intelligence Summaries are contained in F. S. Regs., Part II. and the Staff Manual respectively. Title pages will be prepared in manuscript.

Place	Date	Hour	Summary of Events and Information	Remarks and references to Appendices
BAILLEUL	5/7/16		Showery & wet. 2D	
BAILLEUL/BONNAY	6/7/16		Arrived CORBIE at 12.50 AM. Left CORBIE 4 p.m. arrived BONNAY 8.30 p.m. Fine 2D	
BONNAY	10/7/16		General Routine. Fine 2D	
BONNAY	11/7/16		General Routine. Fine 2D	
BONNAY	12/7/16		General Routine. Fine 2D	
BONNAY	13/7/16		"Zero day" notified for 14th. "Zero hour" 4 AM from which time units would repair to entrain in half an hour. Fine 2D	

Army Form C. 2118.

WAR DIARY
or
INTELLIGENCE SUMMARY.
(Erase heading not required.)

Instructions regarding War Diaries and Intelligence Summaries are contained in F. S. Regs., Part II. and the Staff Manual respectively. Title pages will be prepared in manuscript.

Place	Date	Hour	Summary of Events and Information	Remarks and references to Appendices
BONNAY	14/9/16		"Zero day" slowing tyal to No nurses from 4 A.14	Two 2)
BONNAY	15/9/16		Still at the nurses	1 me 2)
BONNAY	16/9/16		Degree of readiness 1½ hrs	1 me 2)
BONNAY	17/9/16		Degree of readiness 4 hrs	Met. 2)
BONNAY	18/9/16		So on 17th	Oct. 2)
BONNAY	19/9/16		General Routine	1 me 2)
BONNAY	20/9/16		General Routine	1 me 2)
BONNAY	21/9/16		1 NCO 9 ord orderlies to no 5 CCS for temporary ref. due	2)

1577 Wt. W10791/1773 500,000 1/15 D. D. & L. A.D.S.S./Forms/C. 2118.

Army Form C. 2118.

WAR DIARY
or
INTELLIGENCE SUMMARY.
(Erase heading not required.)

Instructions regarding War Diaries and Intelligence Summaries are contained in F. S. Regs., Part II. and the Staff Manual respectively. Title pages will be prepared in manuscript.

Place	Date	Hour	Summary of Events and Information	Remarks and references to Appendices
BONNAY	22/9/16		Capt LUNN & Capt MORAN & 2 men to temporary duty to 38 C.C.S. New Triumph motor cycle received	Warm 2)
BONNAY	23/9/16		General Routine	Fine 2)
BONNAY	24/9/16		General Routine	Fine 2)
BONNAY	25/9/16		Capt DOWNIE, Lt PRINGLE & 15 O.R. due on ambulance 2 light ambulance waggons & one motor car? to Divisional motor par[k] Fahy	Hot 2)
BONNAY	26/9/16		General Routine	Very hot 2)
BONNAY	27/9/16		1 cac O.R. to Divisional workshop Fd. Hos[p]	Hot 2)

1577 Wt.W10791/1773 500,000 1/15 D. D. & L. A.D.S.S./Forms/C. 2118.

Army Form C. 2118.

WAR DIARY
or
INTELLIGENCE SUMMARY.
(Erase heading not required.)

Instructions regarding War Diaries and Intelligence Summaries are contained in F. S. Regs., Part II. and the Staff Manual respectively. Title pages will be prepared in manuscript.

Place	Date	Hour	Summary of Events and Information	Remarks and references to Appendices
BONNAY	28/4/16		General Routine. 1st.D. 2nd.D	
BONNAY	29/4/16		General Picture. 1st.D. 2nd.D	
BONNAY	30/4/16		Two 2nd.D horses from Brigade Head Quarters H.Q. 2nd.D	
BONNAY	31/4/16		Divisional working party returned to 1st and 2nd.D also C.C.S parties	

Wilhm Anson M.C.P

O C 8th Cavalry Field Ambulance 47th

Diary of
8th Cavalry Field Ambulance Vol 20

Month of August 1916.

WARDIARY
or
INTELLIGENCE SUMMARY
(Erase heading not required.)

Army Form C. 2118

Instructions regarding War Diaries and Intelligence Summaries are contained in F. S. Regs., Part II. and the Staff Manual respectively. Title Pages will be prepared in manuscript.

Place	Date	Hour	Summary of Events and Information	Remarks and references to Appendices
BONNAY	1/8/16		Left BONNAY at 6:45 arriving ST PIERRE A BOVY 3 pm	H.ST
ST PIERRE A GOUY	2/8/16		Left 4:30 arriving NEUILLY 12 noon LE HOPITAL	H.ST 2D
NEUILLY LE HOPITAL	3/8/16		General Routine	H.ST
DOURIEZ	4/8/16		Arrived DOURIEZ 2 pm	4 ST
BLINGEL	5/8/16		Arrived BLINGEL 3 pm	H.ST 2D
BLINGEL	6/8/16		General Routine	2D
BLINGEL	7/8/16		Light Ambulance & horses away depot for aug. at R.H.Q. & appointed	2D
BLINGEL	8/8/16		Sports events and kits arrived for Rimoval & permanent billets	W.H.E
BLINGEL	9/8/16		General Routine	H.ST W.H.E
BLINGEL	10/8/16		General Routine	W.H.E
BLINGEL	11/8/16		General Routine	W.H.E

Army Form C 2118

WAR DIARY
or
INTELLIGENCE SUMMARY

(Erase heading not required.)

Instructions regarding War Diaries and Intelligence Summaries are contained in F.S. Regs., Part II. and the Staff Manual respectively. Title Pages will be prepared in manuscript.

Place	Date	Hour	Summary of Events and Information	Remarks and references to Appendices
BLINGEL	12/8/16		Three officers and twenty seven O.R. proceeded for duty to the 44 C.C.S. at PUCHEVILLERS.	WE
BLINGEL	13/8/16		General Routine. H.T.	WE
BLINGEL	14/8/16		Brigade divine service held. H.T.	WE
BLINGEL	15/8/16		Inspection of transport by O/c A.S.C. 3' Cav Div. Wet.	WE
BLINGEL	16/8/16		General Routine. Showery	WE
BLINGEL	17/8/16		Refurnishing wagons commenced. Wet	WE
BLINGEL	18/8/16		Inspection of 10 R Hussars and G Battery RHA by ADMS 3' Cav Div. Fine	WE
BLINGEL	19/8/16		Inspection of Essex Yeo. by ADMS 3' Cav Bde. Fine	WE
BLINGEL	20/8/16		Blankets &c passed through Foden disinfector. O/c & C.F.A visited detachment at PUCHEVILLERS. Fine	WE
BLINGEL	21/8/16		Inspection of R. Horse Guards and M.G.S. by ADMS 3 Cav Div. Fine	WE

Army Form C 2118

WAR DIARY
or
INTELLIGENCE SUMMARY

(Erase heading not required.)

Instructions regarding War Diaries and Intelligence Summaries are contained in F. S. Regs., Part II. and the Staff Manual respectively. Title Pages will be prepared in manuscript.

Place	Date	Hour	Summary of Events and Information	Remarks and references to Appendices
BLINGEL	24/8/16		Returns to home lines, asked, Pard of hospital clears and adm. Fine wre	
BLINGEL	25/8/16		General Routine. Showery wre Order to prepare for move, received	
BLINGEL	26/8/16		General Routine. Fine wre Order to move cancelled	
BLINGEL	26/8/16		General Routine Fine wre	
BLINGEL	26/8/16		General Routine. Orders received for transition. Showery wre	
BLINGEL	27/8/16		Detached (3 Officers 27 OR) returns from 44 C.C.S. Showery wre	
BLINGEL	28/8/16		General routine. Sufford of Orders for home lines Showery wre	
BLINGEL	29/8/16		Y 'n officers 9 ray D.R. to Etaples for details treatment. CAPT H PRINGLE returns from s.b. leave. CAPT J LUMB on s.b. leave to ENGLAND Wet 2d	

WAR DIARY
or
INTELLIGENCE SUMMARY

(Erase heading not required.)

Army Form C. 2118

Place	Date	Hour	Summary of Events and Information	Remarks and references to Appendices
BLINGEL	30/8/16		Received R. in how W.E.F. 20	
BLINGEL	31/8/16		Capt R SLANEY 1 NCO 9 A Other ranks 1 sister and 10 A.V.E.L.U.Y. for duty with motor ambs 8 sent via neco to 47 CCS HESDEN from "en"	Walter Clayton A/Col O/c 85 CFA

140/1787

8th Cav Fd Ambulance

Sept 1916.

COMMITTEE FOR THE
MEDICAL HISTORY OF THE WAR
Date -2 DEC. 1916

Vol 21

Diary of
8th Cavalry Field Ambulance
September 1916

Army Form C.2118

WAR DIARY
or
INTELLIGENCE SUMMARY
(Erase heading not required.)

Place	Date	Hour	Summary of Events and Information	Remarks and references to Appendices
BLINGEL	1/9/16		General Routine. 8 dental cases evacuated to 6/47 CCS for treatment. One ZD	
BLINGEL	2/9/16		General Routine. 6 Dental cases to 47 CCS January 25	
BLINGEL	3/9/16		CAPT J DOWNIE to R.A.E. for temporary m/Skew ZD	
BLINGEL	4/9/16		General Routine. 8 Dental cases to No6 Conv Depot ETAPLES. 15 dental cases to 47 C.C.S. Arrangements made to receive Divisional cases from Brigade. 5 admitted CAPT L.A. MORIN left for ENGLAND on completion of engagement. 10cb 2D	

WAR DIARY or INTELLIGENCE SUMMARY

Army Form C.2118

Place	Date	Hour	Summary of Events and Information	Remarks and references to Appendices
BLINGEL	5/9/16		18 walked cases to 41 C.C.S. Two stretchers returned pro trumpets. Motor bicycle received from O.C. 3 Cav. Div. Supply Column. Wet 2D	
BLINGEL	6/9/16		Medical Inspection of unit. Sent 10 Rev ors to 47 in hospital. 10 walked cases to 47 C.C.S. was notified division HQ move forward 7h 0 after 9th inst. Wet 2D	
BLINGEL	7/9/16		Group relief of Field Inspector Capt J Downie from R.H.S. for Lieut Capt R Slaney 4TOR. 9 one motor ambulance returned from duty with divisional working party, 3 stretcher cases admitted. 10 walked cases to 47 C.C.S. Lone 2D	

WAR DIARY or INTELLIGENCE SUMMARY

Army Form C. 2118

Place	Date	Hour	Summary of Events and Information	Remarks and references to Appendices
BLINGEL	8/9/16		A.D.M.S. letter no. 935 reference to Lieut. Colonel Patrick K. 20 F.A. HESDIN. Brigade letter no. 88—1 received re Brevet Rank on 10.9.16. One officer and two O.R. on duty at Divisional Cornfield. Horse & harness inspection by transport officer. Eight deserters been admitted. Fine.	
BLINGEL	9/9/16		Evacuated all patients to 20 F.A. B.M. 88-4 received. One cow purchased. Ale evacuated. Patients to Brigade. 2 nurse evacuated 15th k 20 FA 2/L 24 GH GRIGNY 7-30 pm	
BLINGEL	10/9/16		Left BLINGEL 12 o/c noon. Arrived BORE starting point 12 o/c noon. Marched via H.Q.S. via HESDIN (Ref. Map ABBEVILLE) arriving 6 pm. Road to DOURIER (w/ Map ABBEVILLE) with sliding that Brigade would probably move about noon on Rec. from Bde. H.Q. 11-9-16. Rec'd A.D.M.S. letter no 941. Line 29 FA k 20 FA 91-24 GH fine.	
DOURIER	11/9/16		Left DOURIER 12 o/c noon and marched to starting point LIESCOURT. 1 km. Marched in Rear of M.G.S. via CRECY — DONVAST to ST. RIQUIER (w/ Map ABBEVILLE)	

WAR DIARY
INTELLIGENCE SUMMARY

Army Form C. 2118

Place	Date	Hour	Summary of Events and Information	Remarks and references to Appendices
St Riquier	12/4/16		Arriving 5 pm. Fine. Roads good. Received BM 94. Rec'd.  Left St Riquier 8 am for clothing point & funds and car of Vaucourt (up of Abbeville). Marched in rear of Q Battery via Ailly-Flexicourt (up Lens up) to St Sauveur. (up of Amiens) arriving 2.30 pm. Rec'd ADMS Z 1866 re Sanitation Z 1866 - A re water. Rec'd BM 95. Rec'd AMS 120. Rec'd DMS Res army 218 - 9.9.16 & P 4-20, & 217.2, Rec'd ADMS Z 1860 Rec'd 3rd C.D. no 4930. Rec'd DGMS 467/3. True. Roads good.	
Br St Sauveur	13/4/16		True. Resting in billets. Camp occupied most insanitary & cleaned up. Rec'd Brigade BM 96 re maps. Sc F/137 Sc 20/52 re own billets ADM3 9.3.97.5.4 Movement order for following day. Fine	

WAR DIARY
INTELLIGENCE SUMMARY

Army Form C. 2118.

Place	Date	Hour	Summary of Events and Information	Remarks and references to Appendices
St SAVEUR	14/9/16		Left St Saveur 9AM in Brigade column following 9 Battery. Route Northern of AMIENS, RIVERY, CAMON to X area No 6 BUSSY ref map AMIENS 1-100000 arriving 12 noon. Forage carts stuff (mostly) blankets remained in town. Rec'd ADMST 1867 & 949; DRO dated 13/9/16; ASC 1604 9/16 85 ADMS letter re C.C.S. of advancy stations in the field. Also asking monthy arrangements for aux't No 594. Brigade BM 150 in army movement order for following day. Time 9 a.m. Roads good.	
"X area" BUSSY	15/9/16		Left BUSSY 9 AM in Brigade column followed B Battery via VECQUEMONT and DOURS to Ratt tram will LA NEUVILLE ref map AMIENS 1-100000 roads very good Heavy section ambulance & field ambulance lodged with others ADMS. 8 PM Brigade order re moves to present area at 20 min notice after 9 AM on 16th Rec'd Brigade No B106 allowing time to 8 AM 9 detail orders of	

WAR DIARY
or
INTELLIGENCE SUMMARY.

Army Form C. 2118.

Place	Date	Hour	Summary of Events and Information	Remarks and references to Appendices
LANEUVILLE	16/9/16		Previewed more S of Rue Jue Colo. Rec'd Brigade BM108/1 attaching hue to 7 AM Reviews in camp. Rec'd Brigade No 11 Can Corps G.S. 233/2 Bnge BM 109, 1st NELSON S.F. RAMC(TC) reported at Ref. from N17 C.F.A & 7 N bigade BM108 June Colo 2D	
LANEUVILLE	17/9/16		1AM Rec'd Brigade BM 109/1 instructions for 17th Left in Brigade Extende. & Clearing & Batt. at 7 AM to S of VECQUEMONT rd O.B DAOURS arriving 9 AM. O.yteeds from brigade Read ADMS Z1886 reported accordingly afterwards studs of tetanus fake g running Roads. Sorry 2D	

Army Form C. 2118.

WAR DIARY
or
INTELLIGENCE SUMMARY.
(Erase heading not required.)

Instructions regarding War Diaries and Intelligence Summaries are contained in F. S. Regs., Part II. and the Staff Manual respectively. Title pages will be prepared in manuscript.

Place	Date	Hour	Summary of Events and Information	Remarks and references to Appendices
VECQUEMONT	18/9/16		General Routine. Heavy rain. Recd. 2145/11, Sc 2505, DRO 17/9/16. 2D	
VECQUEMONT	19/9/16		General Routine. Rain early. Recd. ADMS 990 DRO dates 18/9/16. 2D	
VECQUEMONT	20/9/16		Squad drill. General Routine. Cold. Recd. OZ 1189/1, DRO 19/9/16, SRO 189/9/16, CCRO 19/9/16. 2D	
VECQUEMONT	21/9/16		Squad drill. Notified of div. move N. of AMIENS line. Recd. ADMS 994, MRO (copy), Z 1876, Z 1897, Sc/15-2 Sc 2561, BM 115, CCRO 20/9/16. 2D	

1577 Wt. W10791/1773 500,000 1/15 D. D. & L. A.D.S.S./Forms/C. 2118.

WAR DIARY
or
INTELLIGENCE SUMMARY.

Army Form C. 2118.

Place	Date	Hour	Summary of Events and Information	Remarks and references to Appendices
VECQUEMONT	22/9/16		Left for Bergues starting at 9AM No1 N.Z. VECQUEMONT route LA MOTTE, CAHON, ANIENS, AILLY, PICQUIGNY, passing Sqr R. SOMME to CONDÉ arriving at L'ETOILE at 4PM Bivouacked. Fine Read D.R.O. 21/9/16. Map of ANIENS and LENS 1/100,000	
L'ETOILE	23/9/16		Left at 9AM proceeded with Brigade via BRUCAMPS BONGUEUR, CRAMONE AUZI LE CHATEAU arriving at ROUGEFAY 3.30. Refer map LENS 1/100,000 Roads good. Fine Read A.D.M.S. 993/994	
ROUGEFAY	24/9/16		Left at 8.30 with Brigade via GALAMETZ, MARCONELLE, MARESQUEL arriving at BOIS JEAN at 5PM Bivouacked. Fine; 18M n OR f m 21 C.C.S. Road S.E. Read A.D.M.S. 984	

Army Form C. 2118.

WAR DIARY
or
INTELLIGENCE SUMMARY.
(Erase heading not required.)

Instructions regarding War Diaries and Intelligence Summaries are contained in F. S. Regs., Part II. and the Staff Manual respectively. Title pages will be prepared in manuscript.

Place	Date	Hour	Summary of Events and Information	Remarks and references to Appendices
Bois Jean	23/9/16		Overhauling equipment, general routine. Recd BM 120, SRO 23/9/16, RAMC RO 23/9/16, AO. 19/16. Fine.	
Bois Jean	24/9/16		Cleaning & renewing medical equipment; med/cookhouses & tent.. Recd D.R.O. 25/9/16 Fine	
Bois Jean	25/9/16		Repacking equipment. Baths installed for scabies. Recd G 2080, 2081, 2088 Fine	
Bois Jean	26/9/16		Company drill. Recd S.E.F/180, S.C.F/182, Z 1810/1. Fine	

1577 Wt. W10791/1773 500,000 1/15 D. D. & L. A.D.S.S./Forms/C. 2118.

Army Form C. 2118.

WAR DIARY
or
INTELLIGENCE SUMMARY.
(Erase heading not required.)

Instructions regarding War Diaries and Intelligence Summaries are contained in F. S. Regs., Part II. and the Staff Manual respectively. Title pages will be prepared in manuscript.

Place	Date	Hour	Summary of Events and Information	Remarks and references to Appendices
BOIS JEAN	29/9/16		Routine. Received orders to move from present billets before noon on 30th inst.; SC 2651/1; SC/186; BM/30; Z1891; Z1994/1; BRD 29/9/16; BRD 25/9/16; Ane 2.)	
BOIS JEAN	30/9/16		Left billets at 10 AM arrived BEURAIN Ch. 12 noon via BRIMEUX. Roads good. Ref map ABBEVILLE 10000. Rec'd ADMS Z1910/52; Bde SC 2100; M1550; G.R.O. 26/9/16 Line. 1st W.K. CLAYTON reports for duty to DMS 4th Army. Rd.	

John Downie
Capt. RAMC
O.C. 8th Cav. Fld. Amb.

140/1788

8th Cavalry Field Ambulance

Oct 1916

COMMITTEE FOR THE
MEDICAL HISTORY OF THE WAR
Date -2 DEC. 1916

War Diary
of
No 8 Cavalry Field Ambulance
October 1916

Vol 22

Army Form C. 2118.

WAR DIARY
or
INTELLIGENCE SUMMARY.
(Erase heading not required.)

Place	Date	Hour	Summary of Events and Information	Remarks and references to Appendices
BEURAIN.CH	1/10/16		General Routine. Recd orders to move on 2nd inst. Capt J DOWNIE appointed to command unit. Recd ADMS 1004/1; 7.1913; B.M. 132/8; BM 132/4; BM 135- S.C. 2109; S.C./R.186/1; "Bde R"; C.C.R.O. 31/9/16.	
BEURAIN.CH	4/10/16		Left at 1 p.m. arrived RIMEUX 2.15 PM. Road good. R.C. map ABBEVILLE 1/10000. Recd orders for several manœuvres on gnd met in valley C. of AUBIN Sr VAAST. Byr. Recd ADMS letter re RAMC RO 210. Recd ADMS C'lr re wet. On account of changing billets & no procurement accommodation in new area acc. Lakemos evacuated to No 20. F.A. Officers & O.R. (ordes. with Adv. detachment party)	

Army Form C. 2118.

WAR DIARY
or
INTELLIGENCE SUMMARY.
(Erase heading not required.)

Instructions regarding War Diaries and Intelligence Summaries are contained in F.S. Regs., Part II. and the Staff Manual respectively. Title pages will be prepared in manuscript.

Place	Date	Hour	Summary of Events and Information	Remarks and references to Appendices
BRIMEUX	2/10/16		Divisional manoeuvres cancelled. Attached and named Capt J Lullb for temporary duty to R.H.Guards. Rec'd Z.192B,1020; S.C.2112; D.R.O 10/2/16 Wet 2)	
BRIMEUX	4/10/16		General Routine. Rec'd BAQ 2113/1; S.C. 2119; BM140; D.R.O.3/10/16; BR.0.4/10/16 Wet 2)	
BRIMEUX	5/10/16		General Routine. H.D. Espry to take over M.O. Stracline 7m Squadron Rec'd BM.154/3; SG9440; DR.0,5/10/16. BR.O. 5/10/16 Wet 2)	
BRIMEUX	6/10/16		Capt Slaney took over medical charge of R and L Batt'y R.H.A. Rec'd BM.156/3; C.C. 2140; Wet 2)	
BRIMEUX	7/10/16		General Routine. Rec'd ADMS/216; 2141; 2149/1; 1216; Z192B; Z192/1; BM136/4 Wet 2)	

Army Form C. 2118.

WAR DIARY
or
INTELLIGENCE SUMMARY.
(Erase heading not required.)

Instructions regarding War Diaries and Intelligence Summaries are contained in F. S. Regs., Part II. and the Staff Manual respectively. Title pages will be prepared in manuscript.

Place	Date	Hour	Summary of Events and Information	Remarks and references to Appendices
BRIMEUX	9/10/16		Sua charges 9 & 2 L.D. horses reed. Rec'd SC.2109/1; 248; SCD.5027; C.C.R.O. 9/10/16. Four 2D	
BRIMEUX	9/10/16		Denunification of P.H. & 9no blench harvesting fork send on Rec'd BM147; SC.2148; SC.2142; ADMS1017; DRO.8/10/16 Four 2D	
BRIMEUX	9/10/16		General Rivation Rec'd SC.2153; SC.2157; SC.2106; SC.2113/2 3rd CD. C.Z.M.1 2D	
BRIMEUX 4/11/16			Bd and case of diphtheria treated, transport party formed fredeu. Rec'd DRO. 10/11; BDr 776 2D	
BRIMEUX 11/11/16			Owing to diphtheria in hospital personnel every off isolated hospital closed. Hospital front one O.R. refrorts Rec'd MMisc.SC.2141; Z15.40/3; Z 195.5 Four 2D	

WAR DIARY
or
INTELLIGENCE SUMMARY.

(Erase heading not required.)

Army Form C. 2118.

Place	Date	Hour	Summary of Events and Information	Remarks and references to Appendices
BRIMEUX	15/9/16		Series one of act. Whence - curb - knots - Trench Irment routine. Recd B.R.O. 13/9/16; C.R.O. 13/9/16; D.R.O.13/9/16; E.R.O.13/9/16. Wet	
BRIMEUX	14/9/16		General routine. Recd S.C. 2152/1; A.D.M.S. 1528; Z.1962. Wet	
BRIMEUX	15/9/16		General routine. Recd S.C. 2182. Wet	
BRIMEUX	16/9/16		Third conf. case of diphtheria in village. General routine. Recd S.C. 2156/3. Fine	
BRIMEUX	17/9/16		General routine. Recd BM.167; SC.2188; Z.1962; D.R.O.16/9/16.	

Army Form C. 2118.

WAR DIARY
or
INTELLIGENCE SUMMARY.
(Erase heading not required.)

Instructions regarding War Diaries and Intelligence Summaries are contained in F. S. Regs., Part II. and the Staff Manual respectively. Title pages will be prepared in manuscript.

Place	Date	Hour	Summary of Events and Information	Remarks and references to Appendices
BRIMEUX	5/10/16		CAPT P. SLANEY, R.A.M.C. on special leave to IRELAND Rev. L.H. CLENCH returned for duty vice CAPT E.R. PICKARD	
			General routine	
			Rec'd B.M. 109/5; Z.M62/1; C.C.R.O. 16/10/16; D.R.O. 7/9/16	
BRIMEUX	7/10/16		General Routine	
BRIMEUX	8/10/16		General Routine	
			Rec'd B.R.O. 17/10/16; A.D.M.S. 1049 10/4/5; Z.1908; S.C.2182/1 B.R.O. 29/5/11; C.C.R.O. 18/10/16 & 19/10/16	
BRIMEUX	10/10/16		General Routine	
			Rec'd S.C. 1212; 2203; 2205; A.D.M.S. 1049; C.C.R.O. 29/9/16	

Army Form C. 2118.

WAR DIARY
or
INTELLIGENCE SUMMARY.

(Erase heading not required.)

Place	Date	Hour	Summary of Events and Information	Remarks and references to Appendices
BRIMEUX	28/10/16		General Routine Rec'd D.R.O. 28/10/16. B.R.O. 28/10/16	
BRIMEUX	29/10/16		General Routine Rec'd B.O.e 2212; S.C.2182/1; S.C.2132/2 10ed.	
BRIMEUX	29/10/16		Capt C.M. WILMOTT departed for Hdqtrs Chief Veterinary Officer. Rec'd B.R.O. 29/10/16; S.C.2136/4 wet.	
BRIMEUX	30/10/16		Battery Ivan B. hi 14 EJMOND re infer'mt'n packs Rec'd D.R.O. 29/10/16; S.C.2132/3; Z.1973; Z.1979	

1577 Wt. W10791/1773 500,000 1/15 D. D. & L. A.D.S.S./Forms/C. 2118.

Army Form C. 2118.

WAR DIARY
or
INTELLIGENCE SUMMARY.
(Erase heading not required.)

Instructions regarding War Diaries and Intelligence Summaries are contained in F. S. Regs., Part II. and the Staff Manual respectively. Title pages will be prepared in manuscript.

Place	Date	Hour	Summary of Events and Information	Remarks and references to Appendices
BRUCHE	24/9/16		Marched billets to HESMOND route via BEAURAINVILLE & OFFIN (map ABBEVILLE 1/100000) roads good. Ree'd BM 1739/5.	Fine 25
HESMOND	24/9/16		Cleaning billets & transport. Reg'd 1966; BM 1641; ADMS XN125/1 BDR 2223; BRO 27/10/16 DRO 24/10/16; SC 2132	Wet 26
HESMOND	26/9/16		General Routine. Reg'd BRO 24/10/16; DRO 24/10/16; ADMS 1275/7; N12b SC 2138; SC 2132; BR2;	Fine 27

1577 Wt. W10791/1773 500,000 1/15 D. D. & L. A.D.S.S./Forms/C. 2118.

WAR DIARY
or
INTELLIGENCE SUMMARY.

Army Form C. 2118.

(Erase heading not required.)

Instructions regarding War Diaries and Intelligence Summaries are contained in F. S. Regs., Part II. and the Staff Manual respectively. Title pages will be prepared in manuscript.

Place	Date	Hour	Summary of Events and Information	Remarks and references to Appendices
HESTMOND	29/X/16		General Routine. Received B 1999 SC 2233 SC 2225-1 SC 2244 CCR6 25/10/16 June. RS	
HESTMOND	30/X/16		General Routine. Received B 1932-2 HQ 2247 RM 132-24 Shrury RS	
HESTMOND	31/X/16		General Routine. Captain J. LUMB R.A.M.C. was our temporary Medical charge of R.N.G. vice Surgeon-Major COYNE on leave to ENGLAND. Received ADMSS GRO 211 SC 2132-5 2212-1 DRO 2231 GRO 09/X/16 June RS	R. Davies Cpl R.A.M.C. O/i S.C. 24/A

140/849

3rd Can Div

WAR DIARY
of
N° 8 Can: Field Ambulance
for month of
NOVEMBER 1916

Nov 1916

COMMITTEE FOR THE
MEDICAL HISTORY OF THE WAR
Date -3 JAN. 1917

Vol 23

Army Form C. 2118.

WAR DIARY
or
INTELLIGENCE SUMMARY.

(Erase heading not required.)

Place	Date	Hour	Summary of Events and Information	Remarks and references to Appendices
HESMOND	1/11/16		General routine. CAPTAIN H. PRINGLE RAMC and seven other ranks and one Motor Ambulance proceeded to relieve LIEUT Q. F. NELSON RAMC and seven other ranks doing duty with division at acting party attached 5th Army. CAPTAIN J. DOWNIE D.S.O. RAMC proceeded on special leave to Scotland. One other rank proceeded for temporary duty with convoy. All men of the unit were bathed. Weather fine. Received BM 2866, 2304, 2132-6; SRO 2262 CCRO 31/X/16	QS
HESMOND	2/11/16		General routine. Motor ambulance 11Oa proceeded to tempo stop. Motor Ambulance 1485L reported for temporary duty. Received SC 2249, 2273, BMR O 2/xi/16 CCRO 1/xi/16 Act	QS R. Slavin Capt RAMC 6th 8 C F A

2353 Wt. W2544/1454 700,000 5/15 D. D. & L.   A.D.S.S.J/Forms/C. 2118.

Army Form C.2118.

WAR DIARY
or
INTELLIGENCE SUMMARY.
(Erase heading not required.)

Instructions regarding War Diaries and Intelligence Summaries are contained in F. S. Regs., Part II. and the Staff Manual respectively. Title pages will be prepared in manuscript.

Place	Date	Hour	Summary of Events and Information	Remarks and references to Appendices
HESMOND	3/XI/16		General routine. 1 O.R. reported for duty from T.F. Base Depot Received 3 1913 B.R.O. 3/XI/16 S.C. 2240-5 2225-2 RS	
HESMOND	4/XI/16		General routine 30 walked cases sent to No. 20 G.A. HESDIN for treatment Motor ambulance No 15953 sent to No R.S. Depot with broken crown wheel. Motor ambulance No 9393 returns for temporary duty from No 6 C.F.A. Received S.C. 2296 S.G.O. 9/XI/16 D.R.O. 2263-7 2262 RS	
HESMOND	5/XI/16		General routine Received S.C. 2284 2288 2212-3 B.M. 143-4. RS Fine	

Q. Spairs
Capt R.A.M.C.
O/c 6 C.F.A.

WAR DIARY
or
INTELLIGENCE SUMMARY.
(Erase heading not required.)

Army Form C. 2118.

Instructions regarding War Diaries and Intelligence Summaries are contained in F. S. Regs., Part II. and the Staff Manual respectively. Title pages will be prepared in manuscript.

Place	Date	Hour	Summary of Events and Information	Remarks and references to Appendices
HESMOND	6/X/16		General Routine. 90 OR Machine Gun Squadron Arrived Received CERD 5152 Cdr 2132-9 RAMC OPO 213 ADMS 1041 + 1095 03 AH 2240 WCI	RS
HESMOND	7/1/16		Lt NELSON. G.F. RAMC IVFR on medical charge of squadron Horse transport. 90 men machine gun Sqnd. baths Recd S.C. 2132/10 , 2,152/11 D.R.0.2268	W.I. 2nd
HESMOND	8/4/16		Fourteen ludoc came to HESDIN No 7393 instr on amb to work chp Recd B.M. 170/6 CCRD 4/11/16 DR 2295	W.I. 2nd

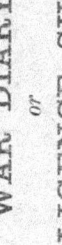

WAR DIARY
or
INTELLIGENCE SUMMARY.

(Erase heading not required.)

Army Form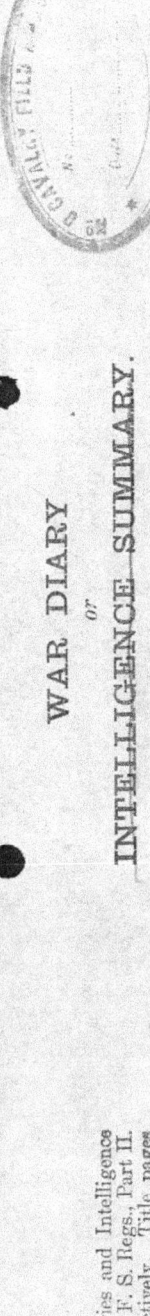

Instructions regarding War Diaries and Intelligence Summaries are contained in F. S. Regs., Part II and the Staff Manual respectively. Title pages will be prepared in manuscript.

Place	Date	Hour	Summary of Events and Information	Remarks and references to Appendices
HESMOND	13/4/16		General Routine Baths 25 men 20th M.V.S. Rec'd 2212/4; 2152/4; CCRO 8/4/16 Capt J Downie from Leave General routine	
HESMOND	14/4/16		General routine. One Officer & OR rank & 9 Other ranks returned from divisional rest & sent to two Inf. Rd. head ccs from R.H.Q. Rec'd G.C. 2351; C.C.R.O. 15/4/16; D.R.O. 14/4/16	
HESMOND	14/4/16		Regimental Routine Rec'd ADMS H/24; H/35; D.R.O. 4/4/16; R&C 2310	
HESMOND	15/4/16		General Routine. 20 men marches 7 oms Cywal & Rec'd Bde M/85; 23 H ADMS M/29; R.O. 15/4/16; Bde M85	

2353 Wt. W2544/1454 700,000 5/15 D.D.&L. A.D.S.S./Forms/C. 2118.

Army Form C. 2118.

WAR DIARY
or
INTELLIGENCE SUMMARY.
(Erase heading not required.)

Instructions regarding War Diaries and Intelligence Summaries are contained in F. S. Regs., Part II. and the Staff Manual respectively. Title pages will be prepared in manuscript.

Place	Date	Hour	Summary of Events and Information	Remarks and references to Appendices
HESMOND	14/9/16		Gomez M.B Egypt Nothers General Rouhui Rec'd RAMC. R.O 214; ADMS H40; CCR.O 13/11/16 Sms 20	
HESMOND	15/9/16		General Rouhui Rec'd G.R.O. 13/11/16; D.R.O. 14/11/16; B.O.C 196 Sms, etc 20	
HESMOND	16/9/16		2.0.2.Lieu M.V.S. Lakes Ohw O.R. reports for duty Lt NELSON B.F. RAMC on 10 days leave to ENGLAND Capt R SLANEY WSK over medical Charge Sic M.F.S Cavalry Brigade home transport. 3rd Cav. Bde Rec'd ADMS H/55; M/44; S.E. M59/2. D.R.O.15/11/16 A.O. front 20	
HESMOND	17/9/16		General Rouhui Rec'd CCR.O 15/11/16 R.A.F.R O.215: D.R.O. 16/11/16 BRO. 14/11/16 Z 14857/2; B.M. 1849 Wed 20	

Army Form

WAR DIARY
or
INTELLIGENCE SUMMARY.
(Erase heading not required.)

Instructions regarding War Diaries and Intelligence Summaries are contained in F. S. Regs., Part II. and the Staff Manual respectively. Title pages will be prepared in manuscript.

Place	Date	Hour	Summary of Events and Information	Remarks and references to Appendices
HESMOND	21/4/16		2.9. Dental car to No 20 F.A. Received Purchase Rec'd BM/84/12. 'S.R 2519'.	
HESMOND	27/4/16		General Purchase Rec'd 134/10. 184/18.	
HESMOND	28/4/16		Field ambulance inspected by D.D.M.S. Cav Corps. Fourteen O.R. 2 horses 1 motor car for R of S with 8" horses battalion. Rec'd BM 184/22. H40/9. H40/6. DRO 19/4/16 June 20	
HESMOND	29/4/16		Capt J LUMB R.A.M.C. 90 men 34 Hundred gun Sgds bathes Rec'd ADMS 1135. June 20	

WAR DIARY
or
INTELLIGENCE SUMMARY.

(Erase heading not required.)

Army Form C. 2118.

Place	Date	Hour	Summary of Events and Information	Remarks and references to Appendices
HESDIN	22/1/16		Capt R SLANEY for leave and return to 3"d C.F.A. Capt H PRINGLE for leave and return ESSEX YEOMANRY. Strength 90 men. 8 horses on exchange. Rec^d S.R.O. 19/1/16: D.R.O. 21/1/16: H/42: S.C. 2328: 2531: 2132/14 B.C. 396: B.M. 113/3/1 : A.D.M.S. 1135	true 20 true 20
HESDIN	23/1/16		NISSEN Hut arrived for reception of sick. Rec^d H/55.	
HESDIN	24/1/16		Evening Routine Rec^d D.R.O. 23/1/16. B.R.O. 24/1/16: S.C. 2338	true 20

WAR DIARY
or
INTELLIGENCE SUMMARY

Army Form

Instructions regarding War Diaries and Intelligence Summaries are contained in F.S. Regs., Part II. and the Staff Manual respectively. Title pages will be prepared in manuscript.

(Erase heading not required.)

Place	Date	Hour	Summary of Events and Information	Remarks and references to Appendices
HESMOND	25/4/16		Lt G.F. NELSON proc'd from leave. Capt R SLANEY referred from 4th CFA. 11 Nurses posted to No 20 F.A. Rec'd A.D.M.S. 1149; 1146; H55/4; Bde M96. kw G.	
HESMOND	26/4/16		General Routine. Prod: C.R.O. 24/4/16; A.S.C. 1782; 3rd C.D. 8572; ADMS 1149; 4/32. G.	
HESMOND	27/4/16		Capt H. PRINGLE left farm and with Escort for Lt NELSON to Lewe Zwaneau. Capt J LUMB to 15th R.B. at Humber. Butler gunner. Selborne yun Squad. Rec'd D.R.O. 24/4/16; Sc. 2341. G.	

Army Form S.

WAR DIARY
or
INTELLIGENCE SUMMARY.
(Erase heading not required.)

Place	Date	Hour	Summary of Events and Information	Remarks and references to Appendices
HESMOND	28/11/16		Cap'n H P PRINGLE for temporary duty 2 H.Q. 24th Div. Bath No 70 men 28th Machine Gun Sqn. Rec'd S.C. 996; S.C. 2392; S.C. 2544; S.C. 2545.	
HESMOND	29/11/16		General Routine Rec'd S.C. 2223/1; B.R.O. 29/11/16; S.R.O. 25/11/16 Z 1975/6; Z 1966/2; A.D.M.S. 1159; B.M. 193/10 A.S.E. 1414	
HESMOND	30/11/16		Bath'd 20 men 20th M.U.S. Rec'd D.R.O. 29/11/16	

John Donovan
Capt. R.A.M.C.
OC 8th Cav. Fd. Amb.

WAR DIARY
of
8th Can. Field Ambulance

December 1916

Army Form C.2118.

WAR DIARY
or
INTELLIGENCE SUMMARY.
(Erase heading not required.)

Instructions regarding War Diaries and Intelligence Summaries are contained in F. S. Regs., Part II. and the Staff Manual respectively. Title pages will be prepared in manuscript.

No 8 CAVALRY FIELD AMBULANCE

Place	Date	Hour	Summary of Events and Information	Remarks and references to Appendices
HESMOND	1/12/16		General Routine. Recd A: 74; H 80; S.S.23354; 173/12 forms	
HESMOND	2/12/16		Capt C.H. WILMOT rets from 5 days Fields Spares 12 dental cases to No 26 F.A. Recd H84; H84; S.S.H. : SBH : 040: 11: SBH : 31337: S22534 D.D.O. 71/12/1. Enamel preparations Capt H PRINGLE returned from duty and was appointed hosty. R.S.	
HESMOND	3/12/16		General Routine Bathed 90 men of W.S. Squadron Lieut Q.F. NELSON returned from surgery duty as to 6 Ross Horseway Two horses A.S.C. M.T. released to 3rd Cav Div Supply Column gone R.S.	
HESMOND	4/12/16			

Army Form C. 2118.

WAR DIARY
or
INTELLIGENCE SUMMARY.
(Erase heading not required.)

Instructions regarding War Diaries and Intelligence Summaries are contained in F. S. Regs., Part II. and the Staff Manual respectively. Title pages will be prepared in manuscript.

Place	Date	Hour	Summary of Events and Information	Remarks and references to Appendices
HESMOND	5/12/16		General Routine	
			Returning 2 horses from stable yard Bullets 40 Rounds 8 th. Sd. S. Spoulsore	
			Received H-68-2 C.C.G 6 4/20/16	
			Suis	R.S
HESMOND	6/12/16		General Routine	
			CAPT A.W. FOREST reports for duty	
			CAPT H. PRINGLE departs for course of lectures at DIVISIONAL AMBULANCE SCHOOL	
			Received H-86 B.M. 173-18 S.C. 23-89 wet	
				R.S.
HESMOND	7/12/16		General Routine	
			CAPT C.M. WILLMOTT departs on 10 days leave to England	
			Received XN 14.1 - 142 D.R.G 6-12-16	
			Fine	R.S

Army Form C. 2118

WAR DIARY
or
INTELLIGENCE SUMMARY.
(Erase heading not required.)

No. 8 CAVALRY FIELD AMBULANCE

Place	Date	Hour	Summary of Events and Information	Remarks and references to Appendices
HESMOND	8/12/16		General Routine. One officer & 8 O.R. sent to A.T.D Etaples for dental treatment. R.S	
HESMOND	9/12/16		General Routine. CAPT. H. PRINGLE returns from Divisional Auth. Gas School. 20 Recruits sent to No. 29 Field Ambulance HESDIN for treatment. Received B.M. 184-28 S.R.O. 4/12/16 D.R.O. 8/12/16 R.S	
HESMOND	10/12/16		General Routine. 1 N.C.O. sent for course of instruction to Divisional Auth. Gas School. Received S.C. 2405. R.S	

WAR DIARY or INTELLIGENCE SUMMARY.

Army Form C. 2118.

Place	Date	Hour	Summary of Events and Information	Remarks and references to Appendices
HESMOND	11/10/16		General Routine 1 L.A. wagon with 2 men returned with H.Q. Essex Yeomanry at PLUMOISON for coaching gear from that regiment and the 10th Royal Hussars to BEAURAINVILLE only. Received S.C. 2609, 2368-1, 2386 D.R.6 11/10/16 Wet RS	
HESMOND	12/10/16		General Routine Capt A.W. FOREST departed on long leave to Scotland. 90 men of the 8th R.B. Squadron billets. Received H 109 H 20-12 Wet	
HESMOND	13/10/16		General Routine O.C. visits billets & the latrine area on Bregoire Aurigny area. Received B-1796-2 Same told RR	

WAR DIARY
or
INTELLIGENCE SUMMARY

(Erase heading not required.)

Army Form C. 2118.

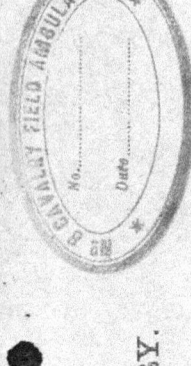

Place	Date	Hour	Summary of Events and Information	Remarks and references to Appendices
HESMOND	13/12/16		General Routine. Recd D.T.O. 13/12/16 Fine	
HESMOND	15/12/16		General Routine. All men bathed. Arrangements for washing men of Bty. Capt J LUMB R.A.M.C on leave to ENGLAND Recd C.C.R.O. 14/12/16 ; Wet -	
HESMOND	16/12/16		General Routine 10192 SERGT MAJOR ARMSTRONG. T. H RAMC ⎱ Awarded Military 60 PTE ☓ HOLLINGS I RAMC ⎰ medal 1124 PTE NUTTING J W RAMC tendrs Gazette4/12/16 Recd S.R.O. 14/12/16 Fine	
HESMOND	17/12/16		General Routine Recd S.C.2153/14 ; Fine	

Army Form C. 2118.

WAR DIARY
or
INTELLIGENCE SUMMARY.
(Erase heading not required.)

Instructions regarding War Diaries and Intelligence Summaries are contained in F. S. Regs., Part II. and the Staff Manual respectively. Title pages will be prepared in manuscript.

No 2 Cavalry Field Ambulance

Place	Date	Hour	Summary of Events and Information	Remarks and references to Appendices
HESMOND	18/12/16		General Routine. Recd Z 1919/2; Z 1884/5; Z 1979/5; H448/4; H1074; H1163; B.M. 184/30; B.M. 187	Wet
HESMOND	19/12/16		General Routine. Recd Z 1624/2; S.C.2421; S.C.2405/1; S.C.2719/1; S.C.2424; S.C.2417	Frosty 2w
HESMOND	20/12/16		General Routine. Recd B.M. 228/c; S.C.2424; S.C.2417 12 men with 6th Provost Bat.	Fine 2w
HESMOND	21/12/16		Twelve O.R. from 8th Provost bat. Recd S.C.2425; S.C.2408/5; Z 1132/5 I 15.46/6; H123; X N 149; D.R.O. 28/12/16	Fine 2w

2353 Wt W2544/1454 700,000 5/15 D. D. & L. A.D.S.S./Forms/C.2118.

Army Form C. 2118

WAR DIARY
or
INTELLIGENCE SUMMARY.

(Erase heading not required.)

Instructions regarding War Diaries and Intelligence Summaries are contained in F. S. Regs., Part II. and the Staff Manual respectively. Title pages will be prepared in manuscript.

Place	Date	Hour	Summary of Events and Information	Remarks and references to Appendices
HESMOND	22/12/16		Lt./Col. HESMOND 9 AM arrived MERLIMONT PLAGE 2.15 took over DRS from 1st C.F.A. transport scouts billets N end of MERLIMONT Rec'd S.C. 2479; S.C.2481. wit and Rec'd S.C. 2479; S.C.2481.	
MERLIMONT PLAGE	23/12/16		General Routine Cap'n WILLMOT C.M. & Cap'n FORREST A.W. returned from leave Rec'd A.D.M.S. 1254; H42/5; H26; B.M. 237; B.P.O. 23/12/16; B.M. 237; B.P.O. 23/12/16 2nd	
MERLIMONT PLAGE	24/12/16		General Routine Rec'd H29; BM 240; D.R.O. 22/12/16; G.R.O. 21/12/16 Army 2nd	
MERLIMONT PLAGE	25/12/16		General Routine Rec'd BM 244; S.C. 491. 2nd Line	

Army Form C. 2118.

WAR DIARY
or
INTELLIGENCE SUMMARY.

(Erase heading not required.)

Instructions regarding War Diaries and Intelligence Summaries are contained in F. S. Regs., Part II. and the Staff Manual respectively. Title pages will be prepared in manuscript.

Place	Date	Hour	Summary of Events and Information	Remarks and references to Appendices
HERLIMONT PLACE	26/12/16		General Routine. CAPt WILLMOT for duty with 3rd Cav Div Supply Col. Recd H 48/5; H 127; S.C. 841; B.M. 244/1.	
HERLIMONT PLACE	27/12/16		General Routine. Recd H 128; B.M. 2457/1; R.A.M.C. R.O. 216; G.C.R.O. 24/12/16.	
HERLIMONT PLACE	28/12/16		Transport section inspected by G.O.C. 5th Cav. Brigade. Inspection Bullets invited by A.D.M.S. 3rd Cav. Div. Recd Z 1152/2/6; B.M. 473/23; D.R.O. 26/12/16; G.C.R.O. 24/12/16.	
HERLIMONT PLACE	29/12/16		General Routine. Recd B.M. 2457/2; S.C. 2908; D.R.O. 27/12/16.	

Army Form C. 2118.

WAR DIARY
or
INTELLIGENCE SUMMARY.
(Erase heading not required.)

Place	Date	Hour	Summary of Events and Information	Remarks and references to Appendices
MERLIMONT PLAGE	31/12/16		General routine. Recd HM9; S.C. 2439; D.R.O. 29/12/16; {wire 2}	
MERLIMONT PLAGE	31/12/16		General Routine. Recd H130; H131; S.C. 2442 {wire 2}	

John Devine
Capt. R.A.M.C.
O C 8° Cav. Fd. Amb.

1-1-17

140/19+1

Vol 25

3rd Aus. Div.

Diary of
8th New Zeal Field Ambulance

January 1917

COMMITTEE FOR THE
MEDICAL HISTORY OF THE WAR
Date 13 MAR. 1917

WAR DIARY
or
INTELLIGENCE SUMMARY.

Army Form C. 2118.

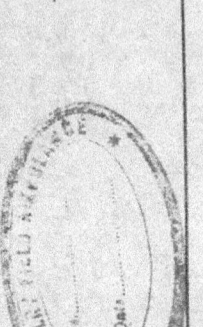

Place	Date	Hour	Summary of Events and Information	Remarks and references to Appendices
MERLIMONT PLAGE	1/1/17		Twelve dental cases to A.I.D. ETAPLES — General Routine Ord A149; Z1690/1; XN158; H149; H136/1; SC2454 SC2953; SC2444/1; DRO 13/12/16 June 2D	
MERLIMONT PLAGE	2/1/17		General Routine Capt J LUMB returns from Leave Prod H138/1; H116; RAMC R.O.2.8; B2&C June 2D	
MERLIMONT PLAGE	3/1/17		General Routine Capt A. PRINGLE on Leave to IRELAND Prod H142; St 2943; S.R.O. 31/12/16 June 2D	
MERLIMONT PLAGE	4/1/17		General Routine Red ADMS 12/12; H129/1; XN142; ASC 1853; 12/14 SC 249; SC 9238/1; DRO 3/1/17 June 2D	

Army Form C. 2118.

WAR DIARY
or
INTELLIGENCE SUMMARY.

(Erase heading not required.)

Instructions regarding War Diaries and Intelligence Summaries are contained in F. S. Regs., Part II and the Staff Manual respectively. Title pages will be prepared in manuscript.

Place	Date	Hour	Summary of Events and Information	Remarks and references to Appendices
MERLIMONT PLACE	5/4/17		General Routine. Rec'd SC.233/5 1/335/3. Zero.	
MERLIMONT PLACE	6/4/17		General Routine. Rec'd H.128/3; H.157; A.D.C.10; B.P.O.6117. Zero. June 20.	
MERLIMONT PLACE	7/4/17		General Routine. Rec'd H.128/2. H.166. H.45/3. S.C.796/3 Zero. June 20.	
MERLIMONT PLACE	8/4/17		General Routine. 18 Mental cases. Strong wind & rain. Rec BM263	
MERLIMONT PLACE	9/4/17		General Routine. Rec'd Z.15/4/10; SC.2984/2; SC.2984; CCRO 6/4/17. Showery.	

2353 Wt. W2544/1454 700,000 5/15 D.D.&L. A.D.S.S./Forms/C. 2118.

Army Form C. 2118.

WAR DIARY
or
INTELLIGENCE SUMMARY.
(Erase heading not required.)

Instructions regarding War Diaries and Intelligence Summaries are contained in F. S. Regs., Part II. and the Staff Manual respectively. Title pages will be prepared in manuscript.

Place	Date	Hour	Summary of Events and Information	Remarks and references to Appendices
MERLIMONT PLAGE	10/1/17		General Routine Recd 2/1594/3; S.R.O. 7/1/17 from 2D	
MERLIMONT PLAGE	11/1/17		General routine Recd H194; H196; S.C.2990; S.C.2991; S.C.2992 from 2D wet. C.C.R.O. 9/17	
MERLIMONT PLAGE	12/1/17		General Routine Recd ASC 1852; S.C.2993; 2998; 2496; 396/3; 396/4; D.R.O. 10/1/17 Wet 2D	
MERLIMONT PLAGE	13/1/17		General Routine Recd S.C.2999; S.C.2371/1; RAMC R.o 219 B.R.O. 13/1/17; D.R.O. 12/1/17 fine 2D	

Army Form C. 2118.

WAR DIARY
or
INTELLIGENCE SUMMARY.

(Erase heading not required.)

Instructions regarding War Diaries and Intelligence Summaries are contained in F.S. Regs, Part II. and the Staff Manual respectively. Title pages will be prepared in manuscript.

[Stamp: No 9 CAVALRY FIELD AMBULANCE]

Place	Date	Hour	Summary of Events and Information	Remarks and references to Appendices
MERLIMONT PLAGE	14/1/19		Normal Routine. Transport Section moved to AIRON ST VAAST. Cap^n R SLANEY on leave to IRELAND. Ref: ADMS 1425-18 R.O 14/1/17; C.C. R.O 12/1/17. Front End	
MERLIMONT PLAGE	15/1/19		Normal Routine. Ref: S.C. 2304; H 182; ADMS 1226. End	
MERLIMONT PLAGE	16/1/19		Normal Routine. G.O.C. 3rd Cav. Div. inspected D.R.S. Ref: C.B. 10 D.R.O 13/1/17. Five colo End	
MERLIMONT PLAGE	17/1/19		Normal Routine. Ref: S.C. 25/14; BH 271; H 121; H 186; R.O 14/1/17; C.C R.O 13/1/17; C R.O 13/1/17. With ends End	

2353 Wt. W2544/1454. 700,000 5/15 D. D. & L. A.D.S.S./Forms/C. 2118.

Army Form C. 2118.

WAR DIARY
or
INTELLIGENCE SUMMARY.
(Erase heading not required.)

Instructions regarding War Diaries and Intelligence Summaries are contained in F. S. Regs., Part II. and the Staff Manual respectively. Title pages will be prepared in manuscript.

Place	Date	Hour	Summary of Events and Information	Remarks and references to Appendices
MERLIMONT PLAGE	5/4/17		General Routine. Rcd Z.1969; H189; SC 2576, 2577 W.d. 9000 2D	
MERLIMONT PLAGE	18/4/17		General Routine. Transfer of photos by OC ASC 3rd Cav. Bde. Rcd BM173/33; SC 2578, 2579, BRO 19/4/17 front 2D	
MERLIMONT PLAGE	20/4/17		General Routine. Use LD Motor cements – Arrange Rcd H185; DRO 19/4/17 front 2D	
MERLIMONT PLAGE	21/4/17		General Routine. Rcd B2 HR1/2 front 2D	

WAR DIARY
or
INTELLIGENCE SUMMARY

Army Form C. 2118.

Place	Date	Hour	Summary of Events and Information	Remarks and references to Appendices
MERLIMONT PLAGE	22/1/17		Received Routine Red BM 243; BM 244; ADMS P41; ADMS P4173; SC 2532; 2533; 2536; 2537 Reinforcements	
MERLIMONT PLAGE	23/1/17		Received Routine Red A48/65; Z 1734; SC 796; BRO. 25/1/17 D.R.O. 21/1/17 Reinforcements	
MERLIMONT PLAGE	24/1/17		Received Routine Red A15-7/2; SC 2573; SC 2560; BR 0 27/1/17 Reinforcements	
MERLIMONT PLAGE	25/1/17		Received Routine CAPT SLANEY returned from leave Rec'd m/194 SC. 2552; SC 2544 Frost	

Army Form C. 2118.

WAR DIARY
or
INTELLIGENCE SUMMARY.

(Erase heading not required.)

Instructions regarding War Diaries and Intelligence Summaries are contained in F. S. Regs., Part II. and the Staff Manual respectively. Title pages will be prepared in manuscript.

Place	Date	Hour	Summary of Events and Information	Remarks and references to Appendices
MERLIMONT PLAGE	26/1/17		General Routine. Read A/199; H/194; H/15-7/2; SC25-46; CB10 ADMS 195-8; SC 2405; 2559/25-48; 25-46; BRO.26/1/17. Issued 20	
MERLIMONT PLAGE	27/1/17		General Routine Read BM1280; DRO 5/1/17; SC 25-54; CCR025/1/17 DRO 24/1/17. Issued 20	
MERLIMONT PLAGE	28/1/17		General Routine Read A/154/1; BRO.24/1/17; BM280/6; BM280/6 Issued 20	
MERLIMONT PLAGE	29/1/17		General Routine Read SC.25-56; BM250/3; SC.543/3; SC476/7; SCM/26/1/17; H/40/221; SC25-48/1	

WAR DIARY
INTELLIGENCE SUMMARY

Army Form C. 2118.

Place	Date	Hour	Summary of Events and Information	Remarks and references to Appendices
MERLIMONT PLAGE	30/4/17		General Routine. Lt NELSON to Cap Jax School Peas BM 260/11; SC 25.56; SC 25.62; SC 1645/1; SC 2360/1.	
MERLIMONT PLAGE	31/5/17		General Routine. Peas + N 163; H/213; Z/1376/4; Z/1738/2; SC 2358/13; SC 2352; H/209; H/208; H/202. Twenty [?]	

John Downe
Capt. R.A.M.C.
OC 8 Cav. Fld. Amb.

3rd Cav. Div.

Vol 26

WAR DIARY

of

No 8 Cavalry Field Ambulance

February 1917.

Army Form C. 2118.

WAR DIARY
or
INTELLIGENCE SUMMARY.
(Erase heading not required.)

Instructions regarding War Diaries and Intelligence Summaries are contained in F.S. Regs., Part II. and the Staff Manual respectively. Title pages will be prepared in manuscript.

Place	Date	Hour	Summary of Events and Information	Remarks and references to Appendices
FRUGES	1/5/17		Left MERLIMONT PLACE at 8 A.M. arrived FRUGES 4 P.M. Road slippery. Read SC.25-43; DRB 31/17; BM184/1	
FRUGES	2/5/17		Usual Routine. Water cart to 8th Cav. Pioneer Bn. Read 4/HG/32; BM184/31. P.38.	
FRUGES	3/5/17		Usual Routine. Lt NELSON to S.A.A. School. Left my 10 P.S.; 1/53-56 S; 12/53-56 S; 10 SC/213 S.P.O?;	
FRUGES	4/5/17		Usual Routine. Read 8 C 25-56 ; 1/53-56 ; H/220 ; DP03 ; 907/H ; 802/H.	
FRUGES	5/5/17		Usual Routine.	

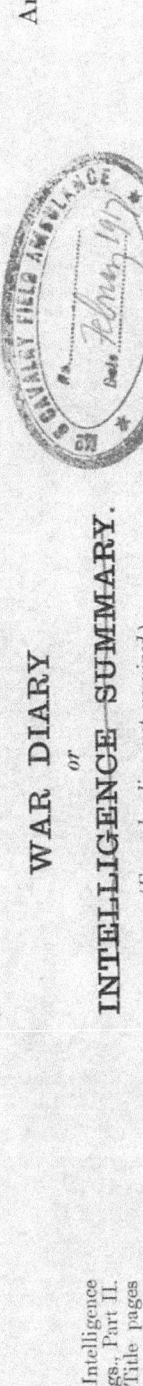

WAR DIARY
or
INTELLIGENCE SUMMARY
(Erase heading not required.)

Army Form C. 2118.

Place	Date	Hour	Summary of Events and Information	Remarks and references to Appendices
FRUGES	6/2/17		General Routine LT NELSON to 4th BdeR HA Read SC25-84/2; 4/124/2; 4/48/20; 4/57/5 SC2132/22; CCROg/4/17; SC25-22	
FRUGES	12/2/17		CAPT FORREST 9 9 R. to 15th Cav-Received tel-Read 05315/3; SC25-75; SC25-76; SC25-78 H/66/2; H/2/1; M/2/12; SC2001; BM/275/4 SC25-79/1 BM/243/5; H/22/4 Yours General Routine Read 4/15-8/5; 7/528/5; 4/129/5; 4/122/1 Thorold 2d	
FRUGES	8/2/17		General Routine Read BM30-0; DRO 8/2/17 Thorold 2d	

WAR DIARY
INTELLIGENCE SUMMARY

Army Form C. 2118.

Place	Date	Hour	Summary of Events and Information	Remarks and references to Appendices
FRUGES	10/2/17		General Routine Orders NCO 1102 from 6th Cavalry Bde Recd M/145; SC 2613; BM 294/5; DRO 15/4/17 CO's & OC's	
FRUGES	11/2/17		General Routine Orders Recd SC 2608; 2607/14 SRO 4th Feb H/226	
FRUGES	12/2/17		General Routine Orders Lt NELSON from 4 Bde RHA Recd H/231; M/225; M/228	
FRUGES	13/2/17		General Routine Orders 2 R.A.M.C reinforcements 9, 1 P.B. man Recd SC 2611; H/232; SC 2613; H/254; M 233; SC 2615	

Army Form C. 2118.

WAR DIARY
or
INTELLIGENCE SUMMARY.

(Erase heading not required.)

Place	Date	Hour	Summary of Events and Information	Remarks and references to Appendices
FRUGES	14/2/17		Emerald Routine Recd H/224/1, 2/235, SC 2605/1 DRO 15th Feb, H/229/1, BM 273/6 Further DD	
FRUGES	15/2/17		Emerald routine Recd ADMS 849, X 185, H/258, CCRO 13575 CC 236/1, H/211/2, SRO 135 Inf, Inver	
FRUGES	16/2/17		Further Read SC 2137/14/1, SC 746/05/5/153 SC 2615/1, Z/14753/1, H/1455/4, CC 2514/1 SC 2620 SC 2414/1, SC 2621, SC 279/14 CAPT A PRINGLE attd ⟨?⟩ RH strength from 1st 2/17 N.O. Cith 24/9/246 (AMD) Adden 3654 Inf	

Army Form C. 2118.

WAR DIARY
or
INTELLIGENCE SUMMARY.
(Erase heading not required.)

Place	Date	Hour	Summary of Events and Information	Remarks and references to Appendices
FRUGES	12/5/17		General Routine Para 4/211/3 4/993	
FRUGES	13/5/17		General Routine Para 496/12. 4/139/2 4/993	
FRUGES	13/5/17		Engineer Routine Para 2/995/2. 4/30/27. SC2338/2 Mules	
			General Routine Para 4/139. SC2615- 4/194/6. BM 311. SC2236. 4/246. 4/295 Mules	
FRUGES	2/5/17		Routine 2 RAMC reinforcements Per S4544. 4268* SC2659. Z/1455/8. 4/247	

Army Form C. 2118.

WAR DIARY
or
INTELLIGENCE=SUMMARY.
(Erase heading not required.)

Instructions regarding War Diaries and Intelligence Summaries are contained in F. S. Regs., Part II. and the Staff Manual respectively. Title pages will be prepared in manuscript.

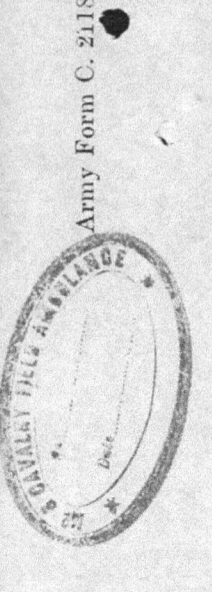

Place	Date	Hour	Summary of Events and Information	Remarks and references to Appendices
FRUGES	22/7/17		General Routine. Ref: SC2662; SC2644; BH294/6; SC249/1. EPO.20 W 245	
FRUGES	23/7/17		General Routine. Recd BH294/7; XN147; RAMC Ro.220; SC2640. Ens Lecture 2D 9643; BMS15 miles 2D	
FRUGES	24/7/17		Lines of Comm. Board me. Ref RAMC 1271. Riding School for Hearers H245/1. Ref 2D	
FRUGES	25/7/17		General Routine. (G) ADMS 1272; SC2653; time 2D	

WAR DIARY
or
INTELLIGENCE SUMMARY

Army Form C. 2118.

Place	Date	Hour	Summary of Events and Information	Remarks and references to Appendices
FRUGES	2/7/18		General Routine. Recd. ADMS/2799 H138/22; H125/23; H125/25 Fine End. Recd ADMS/2794 H138/22; H125/23	
FRUGES	3/7/18		General Routine. Riding School Recd ADMS 12/73; H125 SC 2658. Fine End	
FRUGES	4/7/18		General Routine. Riding School Recd. A249/1; H249; Z1475/8; DH273/6/1 OC 2662. Fine	

John Bourne
Capt. R.A.M.C.
OC 8th Cav. Fd. Amb.

14/2086

Vol 7

War Diary
of
8th Cavalry Field Ambulance

Month of March
1917

COMMITTEE FOR THE
MEDICAL HISTORY OF THE WAR
Date −6 JUN. 1917

Army Form C. 2118.

WAR DIARY
or
INTELLIGENCE SUMMARY.
(Erase heading not required.)

Place	Date	Hour	Summary of Events and Information	Remarks and references to Appendices
FRUGES	1/5/17		Divisional Routine. Inspection of Reinforcements visited by ADMS. Two Ambulance wagons sick to my unit. Recd H264, H273, H274, H263, S.C. 2666	
FRUGES	2/5/17		Divisional routine. Leoture by ADO Officer today School inspection of wagons returned Hobart Mill. Recd 4163/85, H295, ADMS 1569, SRO25/17	
FRUGES	3/5/17		Divisional Routine. Riding School. On Cadre of men etc. from 8th M.G. 3. Recd Z1975/11	

Army Form C. 2118.

WAR DIARY
or
INTELLIGENCE SUMMARY.
(Erase heading not required.)

Instructions regarding War Diaries and Intelligence Summaries are contained in F. S. Regs., Part II. and the Staff Manual respectively. Title pages will be prepared in manuscript.

Place	Date	Hour	Summary of Events and Information	Remarks and references to Appendices
FRUGES	4/5/17		Inspection of personnel by C.O. Church Parade. Rec'd GCD 5334/8; SC 2462/1; H 272/1.	
FRUGES	5/5/17		Fine 2d. Riding school for trainees; Lectures in gas helmet. Route march in g.no helmets. Rec'd H 248; H 249; SC 776/14; SC 2682; SC 2684. BM 299/11; BM 233/12; BM 320/2.	
FRUGES	6/5/17		Fine 2d. Leghorn on /read air to revet.; Riding school for trainees. Capt'n J. Downie proceeded on 10 days leave to SCOTLAND handing over charge of Th. march to Capt'n R. SLANEY Rec'd H 259; H82/3; Z 1425/13; Z 1425/14. P 117.; DRO. 6/5/17 CCRO 5/5/17 Fine 2d.	

WAR DIARY
INTELLIGENCE SUMMARY

Army Form C. 2118.

Place	Date	Hour	Summary of Events and Information	Remarks and references to Appendices
FRUGES	4/3/17		Bathing parade to Mutul Civic sent to 10-20 Feb Ambulance HESDIN for acid treatment	
			Received BQ&SB H281 DQ6 6-3-17 B&R6 7-3-17 Ael An balance HESDIN	RS
FRUGES	8/3/17		Medical inspection of the personnel of the Unit. Two R.S Lance corporals and one L.A wasser returned from 3rd Cav. Brig. Fed horses and one Belgian orderly admitted to B.Q.S. suffering from contusions - also R one Belgian Officer treated for laceration of scalp both result of motor-car accident	
			Received B.W. 294/15 Rear Hock Feor	RS
FRUGES	9/3/17			

Army Form C. 2118.

WAR DIARY
or
INTELLIGENCE SUMMARY
(Erase heading not required.)

Instructions regarding War Diaries and Intelligence Summaries are contained in F. S. Regs., Part II. and the Staff Manual respectively. Title pages will be prepared in manuscript.

Place	Date	Hour	Summary of Events and Information	Remarks and references to Appendices
FRUGES	9/3/17		General Routine. Captain J. Hunt. RAMC returned from duty with RH.Q. and took over command of the unit from Capt. R. Slaney RAMC. Lecture on Gas & drill and march in gas helmets. Rec'd A142/2. H154/11. Z1475/19. Z1475/16. P.203. SRO. 7/3/17. CCRO 8/3/17. Snow and Frost.	V.
FRUGES	10/3/17		General Routine. Cleaning up of billets, messrooms & waggon-parks. Disinfecting of blankets & personnel. Rec'd H.154/12. H.154/13. H.147/2. SC.796/6. SC 2686/2 CCRO. 9/3/17. Thaw & close damp weather.	V.
FRUGES	11/3/17		CO's parade & inspection of personnel. Captain J. Hunt. RAMC departed to course of instruction at Aircourt for School & handed over charge of unit to Captain R. Slaney. RAMC. Captain R. Slaney also took over Company medical charge of RHS. during absence of Surgeon-Major R.M Cowie at course of instruction at Aircourt for Sellen. Rec'd H 200. H 20/2. SE 266. SC 2686/3. Fair weather.	V.

WAR DIARY
or
INTELLIGENCE SUMMARY.
(Erase heading not required.)

Army Form C. 2118.

Place	Date	Hour	Summary of Events and Information	Remarks and references to Appendices
FRUGES	12/3/17		Billeting parade of all ranks of the Personnel. Gunnysacks & Bny school for Horse sector Company drill. Received 3.1758/14. June QS	
FRUGES	13/3/17		Company drill & stretcher drill. 1 N.C.O. included the stretcher bearers of A & B Horse Sun Sun Sector. Received 3.1886/14. 3.1384/17. H.290. H.294/1. S.C. 2486/1. BM 143/64. SR 6 13/3/17. June QS	
FRUGES	14/3/17		Route march of Horse Sector Smoke helmet drill continues. Stretcher drill. Capt. J. Lunt R.AM.C. returned from course at Command for school. I took over command of the Unit from Capt. R. Flower R.AM.C. & So proceeded for a course of instruction at the Div Sun School. Received BM Q43/15. SR6 12/3/17. BM Q43/17. SR 6 13/3/17 CCR 6 13/3/17. June QS	

2353 Wt. W2544/1454 700,000 5/15 D. D. & L. A.D.S.S./Forms/C. 2118.

WAR DIARY
or
INTELLIGENCE SUMMARY

Army Form C. 2118.

Place	Date	Hour	Summary of Events and Information	Remarks and references to Appendices
FRUGES	15/3/17		Medical Inspection of Personnel of Unit. Squad drill and Route March. Captain R. Friar RAMC and one O.R. of unit returned with medical symptoms from duty with 8th Pioneer Battalion. Recd. S.C. 2686/4. S.C. 2704. S.C. 2706. H.256. 2.1475/20. 2.1442/2. 2. 1510/4. 2.1447/2. Issd. Fine.	
FRUGES	16/3/17		General Routine. Town + Aid Lecture on Bandaging & Smoke helmets. Recd S.C. 2686/5. S.C. 2705. S.C. 2710. R.M. 273/16. Company drill with R.M. 277/16. DR.6 15/3/17 Fine.	
FRUGES	17/3/17		General Routine. Cleaning of billets. Unknown bodyguards at ADMS visited of unit and inspected Brigade Rest Station. One of the Rose needles borrowed from R.Kts. Captain R. Nave RAMC returned to duty from Divisional Gas School. Recd. H.258. H.288. B.M. 273/17. TM.53. CCPO 16/3/17. OR.6 17/3/17. ISD.6 17/3/17. Fine.	

2353   Wt. W2544/1454   700,000   5/15   D. D. & L.   A.D.S.S./Forms/C. 2118.

WAR DIARY
or
INTELLIGENCE SUMMARY.

(Erase heading not required.)

Army Form C. 2118.

Place	Date	Hour	Summary of Events and Information	Remarks and references to Appendices
FRUGES	13/9/17		CO's parade & inspection of personnel of Unit. Two Officers & Men YOR. many wounded with Heads & Face wounds respectively. True. Rec'd S.C. 2716 S.C. 2717	
FRUGES	15/9/17		General Routine. Parade & inspection of Rank mounted section. Bathing of personnel of Unit. Section for Officers in Box Respirators. Drill & exercise in P.H. Helmets. Captain J Davie RAMC(T) D.S.O. returned from leave to Rettemoy & took over command of Unit. One G.S. Limbered wagon received to complete establishment. 	
		10.30pm	Received orders from Brigade to be held in readiness to move on rather hours notice. Rec'd S.C. 2715 H 281. H 142/2 True	

WAR DIARY
INTELLIGENCE SUMMARY.
(Erase heading not required.)

Army Form C. 2118.

Place	Date	Hour	Summary of Events and Information	Remarks and references to Appendices
FRUGES	2/5/17		Riding school for teams. Lecture to heads of mounted section. Personnel bagged & heavy section details. Forage cart evacuated to ABBEVILLE. Light ambulance waggon, two men & two horses returned from temporary duty with No.7 CFA. Recd G.R.O. 8/3/17 ; SS 1841 ; SC 2927. Rain.	
FRUGES	5/5/17		Twenty dental cases for treatment 126 Field Amb. Inspection if march in full marching order by O.C. Egyptians served as set cream football packed. Recd H219 ; BM337. Round covers.	

SB. Cavalry Field Ambulance stamp

WAR DIARY
INTELLIGENCE SUMMARY

FRUGES 22/5/17

Medical inspection of Personnel
Rising school for the men
Drills by troop mounted & other – for any stretchers
Stone equipment improved
CAPT G REDPATH (TC) RAMC reported for duty on
No 2 General Hospital

Rec'd H137/3: DRO 21/5/17: Rain Issued

FRUGES 23/5/17

Rising school – horses
Rode out of French huts station with squad of
Bearer section – carrying wounded in stretchers
Rec'd SC2931/2: SC976/14/1: SC-2716/5: ADMS 1320
Z 1008/2: H15/4/4: H307: BRO 23/5/17: CCRO 22/5/17
Rain Issued

WAR DIARY
INTELLIGENCE SUMMARY

Place	Date	Hour	Summary of Events and Information	Remarks and references to Appendices
FRUGES	24/3/17		Reorganization of Field Ambulance by D.G.O. 5th Cav Div. General clean up messroom & wards. Recd ADMS 1321; Z1986/4; BM.594/1; BM396/1/1 answer BM345; BM346 answ; S.C. 2686	
			C/O & June 2nd	
FRUGES	25/3/17		Church parade. C/O inspection. Recd Z1690/1; H35/20; S.C.2695/1; S.C.2757; S.C.2757; S.C.2686/1; S.C.28-44; BM339/1; CCPO24/5n June 2nd	
FRUGES	26/3/17		Notified 1st Cav Brigade would leave present area on 28th inst. & move to Fortiecht. 16 No 24 General hospital Evacuated pr Ambs to field Amb. Recd No 20 Field Amb. Equipment Trackers Recd C.2435; SC 2742; 2743; 2740; 2528; 2656. Z1914/4; 71381/4; H 314. Rain wind Zephyr 2nd	

Army Form C. 2118.

WAR DIARY
or
INTELLIGENCE SUMMARY.
(Erase heading not required.)

Place	Date	Hour	Summary of Events and Information	Remarks and references to Appendices
FRUGES	2/6/17		Billeting parade for work parties amel Advance Showgrounds to here Rec'd SC2745; SC2493/1. SC2544. SC2735/4. SC2545/2 H316:Z 4457/4: B 33073 DRO 26/3/17. SR025/3/17 G.O. of home 26	
FRUGES	3/6/17		Dull – read morning service by Chaplain members Heavy rain & Rec'd SC2735; CCR 037/17 G.O.s June 26	
FRUGES	4/6/17		Medical inspection personnel of unit Route march in rear, seven sworn. Rec'd SC2450: SC2286/7 June 26	

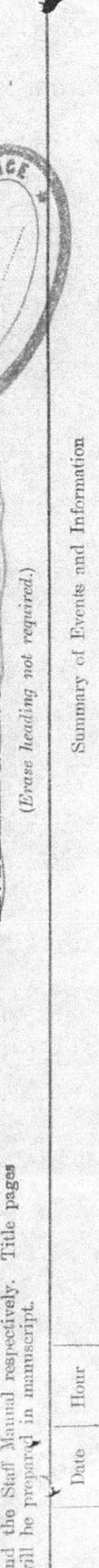

WAR DIARY
INTELLIGENCE SUMMARY.

Army Form C. 2118.

Place	Date	Hour	Summary of Events and Information	Remarks and references to Appendices
FRUGES	2/5/17		Conference ADMS with Brigade Dental Officers Route march — lecture. Recd D.R.O. 29/5/17, B.R.O. 29/5/17, C.C.R.O. 29/5/17, SC 2584/2 B.M. 858/1	
FRUGES	3/5/17		Company and General clean up — bath &c Recd A.M. 258, Z10441, A323, D.R.O. 30/5/17, 3 January 22	

John Downie
Capt. R.A.M.C.
O.C. 2nd Cav. Fd. Amb.

WAR DIARY
of
No 8 (Cavalry) Field Ambulance
for
APRIL 1917

COMMITTEE FOR THE
MEDICAL HISTORY OF THE WAR
Date -6 JUN.1917

B.E.F.

Summary of Medical War Diaries of

8th CAVALRY FIELD AMBULANCE

3rd Cav.Div., Cav.Corps,
3rd Army, from 7/4/17.
till 12/5/17.

WESTERN FRONT 1917.

O.C. Captain J. Downie, D.S.O.

Summarised under the following headings:

PHASE "B": BATTLE OF ARRAS, APRIL - MAY 1917.
1st Period - Attack on Vimy Ridge, April.
2nd Period - Capture of Siegfried Line, May.

B.E.F.

1.

8th CAVALRY F.A.,
    3rd Cav.Div., Cav.Corps,
        3rd Army from 7/4/17.
O.C. Capt. J. Downie, D.S.O.

WESTERN FRONT 1917.
April.

Phase "B": Battle of Arras, April - May 1917.
1st Period - Attack on Vimy Ridge, April.

H.Q. at FRESSIN.

April

- 7th   <u>Moves & Transfer</u>   To FREVENT en route for 3rd Army.
- 8th   <u>Moves</u>   To GOUY.

      <u>Terrain</u>   Roads heavy.

- 10th   <u>Moves</u>   To ARRAS area with Bde. (about H.26.c)

      <u>Casualties</u>   Several in Bde. evacuated to A.P. of 13th B.Rifle Bde.

      <u>Medical Arrangements</u>   "Light and Heavy Sections of Amb. still divisionalised".

- 11th   <u>Operations Enemy, Casualties</u>   Bde. shelled intermittently and by 8 a.m. pack mounted section evacuated 23 W. to R.A.Ps. of R. Bdes.

      <u>Operations</u>   At 10 a.m. 10th R. Hussars and Essex Yeo. went into action over Orange Hill towards Monchy.

      <u>Moves</u>   H.Q. of Unit joined pack mounted section at Copse H.36.c.

      <u>Casualties Horses</u>   3 horses including pack horse K.
                       2   "   W.

      This rendered pack section useless.

      <u>Moves</u>   Later H.Q. to S. of ORANGE HILL.

      <u>Casualties R.A.M.C.</u>   Capt. Wood (M.O. 10th R. Hussars) K.

- 12th   <u>Moves</u>   To RACE COURSE W. of Arras.

      2 p.m. to GOUY.

- 17th   To BARLY.
- 19th   To CHATEAU ROMONT.
- 20th   <u>Casualties R.A.M.C.</u>   Capt. A.A.Watson evac. with Diphtheria.
- 23rd   <u>Moves</u>   To LESPINOY.

B.E.F.

8th CAVALRY F.A.,
    3rd Cav.Div., Cav.Corps,
        3rd Army from 7/4/17.
O.C. Capt. J. Downie, D.S.O.

WESTERN FRONT 1917.
April.

Phase "B": Battle of Arras, April - May 1917.
1st Period - Attack on Vimy Ridge, April.

H.Q. at FRESSIN.

April

7th   Moves & Transfer   To PREVENT en route for 3rd Army.

8th   Moves   To GOUY.
      Terrain   Roads heavy.

10th   Moves   To ARRAS area with Bde. (about H.26.c)
      Casualties   Several in Bde. evacuated to A.P. of 13th B. Rifle Bde.
      Medical Arrangements   "Light and Heavy Sections of Amb. still divisionalised".

11th   Operations Enemy, Casualties   Bde. shelled intermittently and by 8 a.m. pack mounted section evacuated 23 W. to R.A.Ps. of R. Bdes.
      Operations   At 10 a.m. 10th R. Hussars and Essex Yeo. went into action over Orange Hill towards Monchy.
      Moves   H.Q. of Unit joined pack mounted section at Copse H.36.c.
      Casualties Horses   3 horses including pack horse K.
                         2 " W.
      This rendered pack section useless.
      Moves   Later H.Q. to S. of ORANGE HILL.
      Casualties R.A.M.C.   Capt. Wood (M.O. 10th R. Hussars) K.

12th   Moves   To RACE COURSE W. of Arras.
      2 p.m. to GOUY.

17th   To BARLY.

19th   To CHATEAU ROMONT.

20th   Casualties R.A.M.C.   Capt. A.A. Watson evac. with Diphtheria.

23rd   Moves   To LESPINOY.

Army Form C. 2118.

WAR DIARY
or
~~INTELLIGENCE SUMMARY.~~

(Erase heading not required.)

8TH CAVALRY FIELD AMBULANCE.

Place	Date	Hour	Summary of Events and Information	Remarks and references to Appendices
FRUGES	1/9/17		1. On inspection of personnel Church Parade. H51/4, H48/6, SC 794/5, SC 2528/7, B11337/2, BM 267, BM 262, BM 293/5	
FRUGES	2/9/17		Route march - Church coll - tram, SRO 2/9/17, 1994/4/2, BM 544, 2241, SC 2528/7, F846/11, SC 2544, SC 1731/15	
FRUGES	3/9/17		Route march - Continued - harness SC 1753, SC557/5, B0368, H351, DRO 3/9/17, Heavy nunn shower	

WAR DIARY
or
INTELLIGENCE SUMMARY.

Army Form C. 2118.

8TH CAVALRY FIELD AMBULANCE.

Place	Date	Hour	Summary of Events and Information	Remarks and references to Appendices
FRUGES	2/4/17		Equipment Parades CAPT R SLANEY, RAMC & 32 O.R. of Heavy Section to BEAURAINVILLE Rec'd D.R.O. 3/4/17; B.M. 314/1.	
FRUGES	3/4/17		Wed 20 Light M Section left FRUGES 10 A.M. — Arrived FRESSIN 12 non CAPT J LUMB RAMC — attached to Duchess of Westminster hospital Rec'd H 332; H 334/2; B.R. none 234; B.M. 374; S.C. 1768 Br none 234; B.M. 374; S.C. 2768; C.C.R.O. 3/4/17 Showing 20	
FRESSIN	3/4/17		8 C° Parade Rec'd B.M. 374; S.C. 2768; C.C.R.O. 3/4/17 Showing 20	

Army Form C. 2118.

WAR DIARY
or
INTELLIGENCE SUMMARY.
(Erase heading not required.)

8TH CAVALRY FIELD AMBULANCE.

No. ....
Date ....

Place	Date	Hour	Summary of Events and Information	Remarks and references to Appendices
FRESSIN	1/4/17		Left 8.30 AM for Wer starting point Auchy les HESDIN Route from starting point LE PARCQ, WILLEMAN, FLERS, NUNCQ to FREVENT — R-f map LENS 1 – 100000 Roads fair Arrived FREVENT – 4 PM Rec'd Z 1394; H330; BM 163; S.C. 2469; S.C. 2470; S.C. 2757/1 Fair DRO 6/4/17 2D	
FREVENT	2/4/17		Left FREVENT 2 PM Route REBREUVIETTE, LIENCOURT, AVESNES, HAUTEVILLE to GOUY EN ARTOIS arriving 11 PM Roads heavy, fine Rec'd BM 103/1; M 352 2D	

2353 Wt. W2544/1454 700,000 5/15 D. D. & L. A.D.S.S./Forms/C. 2118.

WAR DIARY or INTELLIGENCE SUMMARY

Army Form C. 2118.

8TH CAVALRY FIELD AMBULANCE.

Place	Date	Hour	Summary of Events and Information	Remarks and references to Appendices
BOUY en ARTOIS	9/4/17		Standing by at 2 hrs notice. 3 G.S. waggons & 1 water cart. 1 Personnel with 2 medical orderlies heavy echelon under CAPT SLANEY. F.C. of pack mules & chow forwards with reserve at 10 AM to a point W. of ARRAS approx. Time 12.30. At 4 p.m. forwarded along cavalry track through ARRAS to G.30.a.10.2. Ref map 51B sheet N.3. 1:40000. Remainder of light section left 11 AM & marched by mtd. light echelon of D.69 & 7A.9.d. X roads by Ribaucourt. N. of St. Eve. FOSSEUX under orders of A.D.M.S. 3rd Cav Div. Rec'd orders from A.D.M.S. to bivouac at X rds. W. of M 26. d. 5.5.	

WAR DIARY or INTELLIGENCE SUMMARY

Army Form C. 2118.

8TH CAVALRY FIELD AMBULANCE.

Place	Date	Hour	Summary of Events and Information	Remarks and references to Appendices
ARRAS area	10/4/17		At H.A.M. O.C. of each section with Brigade to CHAMP de COURSES West of ARRAS at 11AM & handing to ARRAS 11.30 returned through ARRAS to attack H.26.c. Ref map 57B.SW.3 2/40000 about 6 PM were forward to H.34 central here Brigade was moved for the night. Several Germans in the Brigade consolidated are of Brigade and 8th K.R.H. Brigade in attack 9 Henry returns of Ambulance etc furnished. Weather cold with snow showers. J.D.	

Army Form C. 2118.

WAR DIARY
or
INTELLIGENCE SUMMARY.
(Erase heading not required.)

Instructions regarding War Diaries and Intelligence Summaries are contained in F.S. Regs., Part II. and the Staff Manual respectively. Title pages will be prepared in manuscript.

8TH CAVALRY FIELD AMBULANCE.
No............
Date............

Place	Date	Hour	Summary of Events and Information	Remarks and references to Appendices
H34 Central R/map 51B 1-40000	11/4/17		Brigade shelled in transit with 9 big SAH [HA?] + K movements. Column crossed 23 a.m. this to regimental ad[vance?]. 36 Rifle Brigade. About 10 AM the 10 Hussars + Essex Yeomanry went into action on ORANGE HILL. Bombay MONCHY. OC SVCFA joined Brigade Headquarters on ORANGE HILL followed by pack mounted section. Shortly after this Brigade Headquarters moved forward to hand in N° 6 & nummy SE of MONCHY. Relant here BRIG GENERAL C.R. BULKELEY JOHNSON killed. Headquarters moved back at O.C. SVCFA then joined the pack mounted section + was by the copse in H.36.C. Horse Trees Ambulances advancing the pack horse were killed. Having a few wounded awaiting Report section walked R.Z. Then came truck with	

2353 Wt. W2514/1454 700,000 5/15 D.D.&L. A.D.S.S./Forms/C. 2118.

WAR DIARY
or
INTELLIGENCE SUMMARY

(Erase heading not required.)

Army Form C. 2118.

8TH CAVALRY FIELD AMBULANCE

Place	Date	Hour	Summary of Events and Information	Remarks and references to Appendices
			handed over reported to Lt Col Lord Tweedmouth who had resumed temporary command of Brigade. He also reported to the attention through Brigade Signals to ADMS 3rd Cav. Div.

Late headquarters were re-established S of ORANGE HILL.

About 3 PM O.C. 8th C.F.A. to find Retention of wounded went into MONCHY.

He found CAPT STORK represented No 8 Sqn too wounded to be there, CAPT WOOD represented No 1 & R Horse had been shelled & that he was carrying the work & that He also found MAJOR COWIE M.O. of the 1st H GUARDS & 2 Nursing himself as to the location of the wounded.

He represented these to the officer in charge of the divisional stretcher carriers & arranged between them as to the picking up & taking out of | |

Brigade H.Q.RS
CAPT G REDPATH of the 9th A.T. mounted section
reported sick at advanced dressing station.
He was evacuated to No 19 CCS
Remainder of light section & heavy section
at field ambulances.
Snow rain & colder

Army Form C. 2118.

8TH CAVALRY FIELD AMBULANCE.

No. ....
Date ....

WAR DIARY
or
INTELLIGENCE SUMMARY.

(Erase heading not required.)

Instructions regarding War Diaries and Intelligence Summaries are contained in F. S. Regs., Part II. and the Staff Manual respectively. Title pages will be prepared in manuscript.

Place	Date	Hour	Summary of Events and Information	Remarks and references to Appendices
ORANGE HILL area	12/4/17		After midnight O.C. 9 Field Ambulance received orders to CHAMP de COURSES west of ARRAS. At 2 PM moved further back to Gouy en ARTOIS preceded by light section personnel & vehicles. Cars two ED	
GOUY en ARTOIS	13/4/17		Standing by at 4 hours notice. 2 L.D.'s over received. Heavy rain all afternoon (see near W.R.O. 13/4/17, SC 2742; SC 2773; SC 2744; also 9 cars) ED	

1577 Wt. W10791/1773 500,000 1/15 D. D. & L. A.D.S.S./Forms/C. 2118.

WAR DIARY or INTELLIGENCE SUMMARY

Army Form C. 2118.

8TH CAVALRY FIELD AMBULANCE

Place	Date	Hour	Summary of Events and Information	Remarks and references to Appendices
Gouy en ARTOIS	14/4/17		Standing by at 4 hours notice. Overhauled equipment. Indent change of issue Lemons nos & ice ? Hessents taken over by men. Recd T.12. J. R.O. 11/4/17; C.C.R.O 11/4/17 col. 2D	
GOUY	15/4/17		Standing by at 4 hrs notice. Heavy elephant returned to road. B.D. Wagner read. Recd S.C. 24/78; S.C./R22; XN 182; XN 183; B.H. 116 ; 1866/3; D.R.O. 14/4/17; wd. 2D	
GOUY	16/4/17		Brigr's Lichen left. 8AM for new billeting area. D.O.K in operator inefficient. Recd B1117/1; T 16; BM 117/e; SC 2789. Temporary Dep. G. No 47 CCS. June 2D	

Army Form C. 2118.

WAR DIARY
or
INTELLIGENCE SUMMARY.
(Erase heading not required.)

Instructions regarding War Diaries and Intelligence Summaries are contained in F. S. Regs., Part II. and the Staff Manual respectively. Title pages will be prepared in manuscript.

8TH CAVALRY FIELD AMBULANCE.

Place	Date	Hour	Summary of Events and Information	Remarks and references to Appendices
GOUY EN ARTOIS	17/4/17		Left at 10AM. Route via man DOULLENS—ARRAS road to BARLY. Refugees LENS 1—100000 Rough going. Rec'd H346; H347; H345; BH127/4; SC 2784/2; ADMS 1340. Snow & hail.	
BARLY	18/4/17		Capt A.A. WATSON RAMC reported for duty. Withdrawal of Equipment & transport returned. Rec'd SC 776; SC 286; SC 25.907; SC 2795/1; AF I; ADMS 4/077. Z 1650/4. Wet.	

Army Form C. 2118.

WAR DIARY
or
INTELLIGENCE SUMMARY.
(Erase heading not required.)

Instructions regarding War Diaries and Intelligence Summaries are contained in F. S. Regs., Part II and the Staff Manual respectively. Title pages will be prepared in manuscript.

8TH CAVALRY FIELD AMBULANCE.
No...................
Date...................

Place	Date	Hour	Summary of Events and Information	Remarks and references to Appendices
BARLY	19/6/15		Lft. 7.30 AM march AUXI-LE-CHATEAU road DOURIEZ, MAINTENAY To CHATEAU-ROMONT (Reno 1-100000) (ABBEVILLE 1-1/1000000) Road heavy. Rec'd ADMS 1397; 1350; 1351; 1352; 1353; 1354 Line 2-D	
CHATEAUY ROMONT	20/6/15		CAPT A.A. WATSON to isolation hospital ETAPLES with diphtheria. Enemy helps; - inspecting wagons M.O. and inspection of men. Rec'd P.253. & Wire 2486/1: S.C.2544; F.N.26 Line 2-D	

1577 Wt.W10791/1773 500,000 1/15 D. D. & L.   A.D.S.S./Forms/C. 2118.

WAR DIARY
or
INTELLIGENCE SUMMARY

(Erase heading not required.)

Army Form C. 2118

Instructions regarding War Diaries and Intelligence Summaries are contained in F.S. Regs., Part II. and the Staff Manual respectively. Title Pages will be prepared in manuscript.

8TH CAVALRY FIELD AMBULANCE.
No. ....
Date ....

Place	Date	Hour	Summary of Events and Information	Remarks and references to Appendices
CH ROMONT	21/4/17		CAPT G. Rice DRAT H. Mohammed to Conf. Hosptial of firm J. Recd S.C. 2/116/1; S.C. 274 c/1; BM 8; S.C. 279 M H 333; H 30/2/1; Z 170/17 Juice 2D	
CH ROMONT	22/4/17		General Routine. Recd S.C. 472/21; S.C. 2804; S.C. 2802 S.C. 279 G/1; S.C. 2556; H21; H 360; BM 10 A F 24 10.10 G.M.N. 20	
CH ROMONT	23/4/17		Left at 1.10 p.m. for L'ESPINOY arrived 2.30 p.m. Recd S.C. 456/22; Z 1340/8; H 135; G.R.O. 30/4/17 Juice Dicoius 2D	

1875 Wt. W593/826 1,000,000 4/15 J.B.C. & A. A.D.S.S./Forms/C. 2118.

WAR DIARY
or
INTELLIGENCE SUMMARY

(Erase heading not required.)

Army Form C. 2118

8TH CAVALRY FIELD AMBULANCE.

Place	Date	Hour	Summary of Events and Information	Remarks and references to Appendices
LESPINOY	24/4/17		Opened Hospital. Inspection of camping up. Recd H1317; H1380; S.C.2801;2810, 2811;2812 B.M.13; S.C.2817; S.C.2775/2; S.C.726/14/2. Line ZD	
LESPINOY	25/4/17		Evacuens Routine. Recd B.J.S.; B.R.O.-25/4/17; D.R.O. 25/4/17. Line ZD	
LESPINOY	26/4/17		P.C.A.38. TC Cav Div received from notes. Route March. Recd S.C. 2822; S.C.797/22; S.C. 2821; H552/2; Z1540/9; B.9/7; H369; BM12/1; H359. Line ZD	

WAR DIARY
or
INTELLIGENCE SUMMARY
(Erase heading not required.)

Army Form C. 2118

8TH CAVALRY FIELD AMBULANCE.

Place	Date	Hour	Summary of Events and Information	Remarks and references to Appendices
LESPINOY	27/4/17		Bath parade & drill. Route march. Recd H.1379; 1910; 1901; M10; SC 2828. B.R.O. 27/4/17; D.R.O. 26/4/17. Line 2D	
LESPINOY	28/4/17		Cleaning up of billets. Recd M888; B.R.O. 28/4/17. Line 2D	
LESPINOY	29/4/17		D.G.O. Parade. Church Parade. 2405- Body of Pioneer 706 D. DOOLEY, Royal Irish Fusiliers accidentally killed on railway, taken charge of. Recd H.1473; S.C. 2834; 2835; 2835; 2837. S.R.O. 28/5/17; D.R.O. 28/4/17. Line 2D	

WAR DIARY
or
INTELLIGENCE SUMMARY

Army Form C. 2118

8TH CAVALRY FIELD-AMBULANCE.

Place	Date	Hour	Summary of Events and Information	Remarks and references to Appendices
LE PINDY	30/4/17		Honor — 638 Pte D. DOOLEY Roy. 20 Fusiliers, Right & Ring wound left at 2 pm for CHATEAU ROMONT on O.R. sent to nearest hosp ABBEVILLE for course of Salversan. Rec'd D.R.O. 29/4/17 ; S.C. 2509/1 S.C. 2843. Time 2.0 John Downie Capt. R.A.M.C. O.C. 8th Cav. F.A. Amb.	

30-4-17

WAR DIARY

of

Nº 8 Cavalry Field Ambulance
for the month of

MAY 1917

COMMITTEE FOR THE
MEDICAL HISTORY OF THE WAR
Date 10 JUL. 1917

B.E.F.

Summary of Medical War Diaries of

8th CAVALRY FIELD AMBULANCE

3rd Cav.Div., Cav.Corps,
3rd Army, from 7/4/17.
till 12/5/17.

WESTERN FRONT 1917.

O.C. Captain J. Downie, D.S.O.

Summarised under the following headings:

PHASE "B": BATTLE OF ARRAS, APRIL - MAY 1917.
1st Period - Attack on Vimy Ridge, April.
2nd Period - Capture of Siegfried Line, May.

B.E.F.

8th CAVALRY F.A.,
   3rd Cav.Div., Cav.Corps,
      3rd Army till 12/5/17.
O.C. Capt. J. Downie, D.S.O.

WESTERN FRONT 1917.
May.

Phase "B": Battle of Arras, April - May 1917.
2nd Period - Capture of Siegfried Line, May.

H.Q. at LESPINOY.

May
- 1st/11th   Operations R.A.M.C.   Routine.
- 12th   Moves & Transfer. To GUIGNY en route for 4th Army.

B.E.F.

8th CAVALRY F.A.,
   3rd Cav.Div., Cav.Corps,
      3rd Army till 12/5/17.
O.C. Capt. J. Downie, D.S.O.

WESTERN FRONT 1917.
May.

Phase "B": Battle of Arras, April - May 1917.
2nd Period - Capture of Siegfried Line, May.

H.Q. at LESPINOY.

May
- 1st/11th   Operations R.A.M.C.   Routine.
- 12th   Moves & Transfer. To GUIGNY en route for 4th Army.

Army Form C. 2118

WAR DIARY
or
INTELLIGENCE SUMMARY
(Erase heading not required.)

Instructions regarding War Diaries and Intelligence Summaries are contained in F. S. Regs., Part II. and the Staff Manual respectively. Title Pages will be prepared in manuscript.

8TH CAVALRY FIELD AMBULANCE.
No............ Date............

Place	Date	Hour	Summary of Events and Information	Remarks and references to Appendices
RONSOY C.H.	1/5/17	2 P.M.	M.O. went & inspected billets at ROISEL & VILLERS	2 Drawn
			Route march	
				Line
TINCOURT C.H.	2/5/17	10 AM	2nd Lt. G.F. NELSON, R.A.M.C. posted to duty (relieves 3rd Cav. D.)	2.)
		3 P.M.	Stretcher drill	
		5 P.M.	Route march	
RONSOY C.H.	3/5/17	9 AM	Medical inspection of personnel	
		9.30 AM		
		6 PM	On reopening ref: inspection 1 sick	2.)
			2nd Lt. G.F. reinf. transferred from Cas. to establishment	
			vice 2.Lt. R. transferred to transport section	
TINCOURT C.H.	4/5/17	7.30	stretcher drill	
		2 P.M.	Stretcher drill	2.)
				Line

Army Form C. 2118

WAR DIARY
or
INTELLIGENCE SUMMARY

(Erase heading not required.)

Instructions regarding War Diaries and Intelligence Summaries are contained in F. S. Regs., Part II. and the Staff Manual respectively. Title Pages will be prepared in manuscript.

8TH CAVALRY FIELD AMBULANCE.
No.............
Date............

Place	Date	Hour	Summary of Events and Information	Remarks and references to Appendices
REMONT CH	5/5/17	9h.	General clean up of billets	
REMONT CH	6/5/17	11 AM	Squadron roll γ inc	(2)
			C.I. parade	(2)
			Church parade γ inc	
REMONT CH	7/5/17	7.30 9 AM	Stables roll	
			Boy separates + whether + small γ inc	(2)
REMONT CH	8/5/17	9.30	Stables drill	
			Afternoon fatigues	(2)

WAR DIARY
or
INTELLIGENCE SUMMARY
(Erase heading not required.)

Army Form C. 2118

8TH CAVALRY FIELD AMBULANCE

Place	Date	Hour	Summary of Events and Information	Remarks and references to Appendices
BOMONT C.H.	9/5/17 10/5/17	2.30	Bathing in forenoon. Elastics drill. Fine	2)
BOMONT C.H.	11/5/17		Received the warning orders for move on 12/5/17. Fine	2)
ROMONT: C.H.	11.5.17.		Carried out duty & took over Command of 8. C.F.A. from Col. Bowman R.A.M.C. (P). Capt. Harry R.A.M.C. (T.C.) left for Interior of Lt. Col. Rowan. I.A. hour before from Divisional Vet. Captain. D.H.V. Scoles on contact. I.A. hour before from Divisional Vet.	(P)
ROMONT: C.H.	12.5.17.		Marched to GUIGNY, distance of 16 kilos about. Left yesterday. Past Albreville 7 am 100,000. Divisional HdQrs. S.c.f. H.C.os 7 m.c. left yr. BEAUREINVILLE in lorries. Received marching orders yr. 13. 9 forenoon.	(P)
GUIGNY.	13.5.17.		Marched to VAULX. B°Echelon marching parade's under Capt. FORREST. Brigade Rendezvous 11.30: Marched via FREMBREAUCOURT – CHERIENNE – FONTAINE L'ETATON. H.D. GENNE-IVERGNY. Arrived VAULX 3.30 P.M. Reg. march 105,000 kms.	(P)
VAULX	14.5.17.		Marched to FROHEN-LE-GRAND. Ambulance about 12 kilos. Brigade Rendezvous 11.36. Marched via ROATHIE – AUXI-LE-CHATEAU – HAYANS - arrived FROHEN LE GRAND 2.0 P.M. via Budd H. F. R. AUTHIE – SEYMOUR commanded J. Brigade commenced on some men of the Regt. That Brigadier-General SEYMOUR commanded, J. Brigade, commenced on some men of the Regt. thus were paraded away in G.S. wagon, after Capt. Pervert Town and arrived at dubranch – three were paraded away in G.S. wagon. good hair ran on tomorrow's march. Brig. Rendezvous HEM 9.25. Marched to TALMAS about 20 kilos. Brig. Rendezvous HEM 9.25.	(P)
FROHEN LE-GRAND.	15.5.17.		Marched to TALMAS about 20 kilos. Brig. Rendezvous HEM 9.25. Arrived TALMAS. 12.45. BERNAVAL – LaVicogne – Pot ang - Torques Lens. Marched via GEZAINCOURT –	

Army Form C. 2118

WAR DIARY
or
INTELLIGENCE SUMMARY

(Erase heading not required.)

Instructions regarding War Diaries and Intelligence Summaries are contained in F.S. Regs., Part II. and the Staff Manual respectively. Title Pages will be prepared in manuscript.

8TH CAVALRY FIELD AMBULANCE
No............... Date...............

Place	Date	Hour	Summary of Events and Information	Remarks and references to Appendices
TALMAS.	16.5.17.		Marched to PONT NOYELLES. about 15 kilos. Brigade Rendezvous Cross junction N.W. of Villers Bocage 9.40 a.m. marched via MOLLIEN-AU-BOIS - ST GRATIEN - QUERRIEU. Arrived PONT NOYELLES 1.30 p.m. Ref. map 100,000 LENS + 100,000 AMIENS. Raining. Spent night. Billets poor.	
PONT NOYELLES.	17.5.17.		Marched to HAMEL. about 12 kilos. Brigade Rendezvous Cross junction N.E. of PONT NOYELLES 9.45 a.m. marched via DAOURS - FOUILLOY - HAMELET. arrive HAMEL 1.30 p.m. Refs. maps 100,000 AMIENS.	
HAMEL.	18.5.17.		Captain G.H.J. Davis RAMC(TC) joined this Unit CMA. for duty. Off to further men today. Vernon Davis etc: Patients sent to O.C. Brigade Box Respirator drill 2 to 6 p.m. Captain Forrest Anwte to 10th Hussars for instruction. M.O.'s March to view J. Kee's H.Q. Captain Wood 980 or Lieut. (Rachael) B.M. 34 4th R.R. Day & 9.25 a.m. (Received orders) found roads S.P.	G.186.
HAMEL	19.5.17.		Marched into bivouacs at BUIRE. Brigade rendezvous township road near BUIRE 6.0 p.m. CERISY GAILLY branch route HERICOURT - CRUIGNOLLES - GEOISMESS - DOMPIERRE PORCELLES ref: map of AMIENS 100,000 Long + Bray. arrived BUIRE 6.0 p.m. PERONNE - DOINGT. 9.45 bivouac Bivouac - DOINGT. arrived B.M. 44/1 rather at PERONNE. Brigade Preliminary spl. order B.M. 44/1. Good camping ground. Received Brigade Suppy G.186 circular. B.M. 34 + 9th Cav. Div. Sir G. 186 circular. Captain Nelson Proceeds Hofspools assume Forces Supply Off. where he has been Serving.	
BUIRE.	20.5.17.		Went over equipment, medical panniers, etc: quakerwanders stores etc: take rather to Palissine washonings. G.S. wagons, clothing. Etc. viewed as soon as possible. Attended conference at Brigade Headquarters. The Brigade to act present in reserve. To 6th + 7th Brigades Gors and Rounds 23.5.24. from youth direction. Medical arrangements mostly retains in hands T. Davisson. Received orders from A.D.M.S. to hospital heavy sicken of ambulance Emergency cases of for a few days. D.R.S. 1st walker Hospital. To Gouy-l'Evèque S & th Divison.	

1875 Wt. W593/826 1,000,000 4/15 J.B.C. & A. A.D.S.S./Forms/C. 2118.

WAR DIARY or INTELLIGENCE SUMMARY

Army Form C. 2118.

8TH CAVALRY FIELD AMBULANCE

Place	Date	Hour	Summary of Events and Information	Remarks and references to Appendices
BUIRE	21.5.17		Heavy Lectr. Cap RO for DOING under Captain Davis RAMC(TC) 4 B.ORs. 1 3.F.Sc. wagons, 1 water cart & 1 milk ambulance. Pte Levy 6 B.Ops sent to Hospital. Sent to Rothschild horse & harness to H.H.S. Went from DADMS who states that in all probability the C.F.A. will not be used for a week or more, ten probably as an A.D.S.	
BUIRE	22.5.17		Wet. Day in lines. Exercised horses in morning to Rear horse. Pte Patrott left for Leave. Review & Sgt's Parade afternoon. Preliminary Dn'n order for relief received by mdg. Marked in pencil line from Bray de S. Capt. Respatt RAMC (TC) put in for transfer to Yeomanry Sanitaire.	
BUIRE	23.5.17		Fine and hot. Inoculation parade to take over 1 Fld. amb. T. Broke on Cpl. Ho Nash Cort with 28 NCOs Cav: Corps. Reconnaissance. Left to Relief for medical arrangements.	
BUIRE	24.5.17		Received Fld. assignments Cav: Cps. Operations No. 5. Inspected San. arrangements of Brigade Hqrs & G. Battery. Major Ridout RAMC(TC) sent in application for transfer. informed ADC v DC what was arranged. Captain Ridout RAMC(TC) sent M. Popkin to O. 2 bars, 1 O Rainbow. S. Guard Mershon satisfactory	
BUIRE	25.5.17		Medical inspection of unit 9.30. Chief Inspection.	
BUIRE	26.5.17		Pte Haas went on Leave. 1 Horse on recognizance. Went Henry section at D.I.R.S & inspected Klein Kamfort. Horses looking well. Party of 1 W.H.O.O. & 13 men deputed to MILLERS RAVINE to work on dug-outs. Seen for ADRS over. Capt. O W. to R. Pescore Parte to Sanitaire, satisfactory.	
BUIRE	27.5.17			
BUIRE	28.5.17		Inspection Rothschild R/5 B. P. Ienard, Jogs trips used specifically in most cases. Inspection horses H Hospital Sgt Austin satisfactory. Wrote to R.O. of Captain about Bde. Sc. measure group.	
BUIRE	29.5.17		Capt. Nah remove to N.O. Eaton Germany. Capt. Respatt relieves Lt. died in medical charge of Regt. Lieutenant Seward sent to 36 CCS suffering from shilles never his absence.	

Army Form C. 2118.

8TH
CAVALRY
FIELD AMBULANCE.
No............
Date............

WAR DIARY
or
INTELLIGENCE SUMMARY.

(Erase heading not required.)

Instructions regarding War Diaries and Intelligence Summaries are contained in F. S. Regs., Part II. and the Staff Manual respectively. Title pages will be prepared in manuscript.

Place	Date	Hour	Summary of Events and Information	Remarks and references to Appendices
BURE.	30.5.17.		Visited the Dressing Station of 2 PEHY & the Regtl Aid Post in B2 section. Capt. Pillans R.A.M.C. reported his arrival and re-takes over his duties.	
BURE.	31.5.17.		Visit by Cookery Expert of 2nd Army who advocates the use of a diet menu. Issued instructs Cooks on saving of dripping etc.	
BURE	1.6.17			

J.P.Collet
Capt. R.A.M.C.

31/5/17

MC/2230

No. 8. Cav. F. A.

June 97.

COMMITTEE FOR THE
MEDICAL HISTORY OF THE WAR
Date −7 AUG.1917

WAR DIARY
8th C.F. Amb
month of June 1917

Vol 30

WAR DIARY or INTELLIGENCE SUMMARY

Army Form C. 2118.

8TH CAVALRY FIELD AMBULANCE.

Place	Date	Hour	Summary of Events and Information	Remarks and references to Appendices
BUIRE	1.6.17		Regt: Sqns. R.H.Gs. B.H.S. & 13 Sqn: T.R.H. left for Remounts. Bg: Comrie R.H.S. H.O./C.	(1)
	2.6.17		Capt: Wood M.O. H.R.H. Returns from leave.	(2)
	3.6.17		Visited D.A.D.M.S at Villers-Faucon, re security of affairs of the unit. Reconnoitered Captain Jarvis' Ramc To be fitted for a CCS. & Stationary Hospital.	(3)
	4.6.17		Captain Hurrey Ramc Tc left for duty at D.R.S.	(4)
	5.6.17		Nothing to Report	(5)
	6.6.17		Inspection R.H.G. Braedon. Lewis Gun with Greige Coyts. & had a run to the ruins. Return rest complete.	(6)
	7.6.17		Inspected Foundations. R: E. B. Loomis. please had a mis-adventure. Sub a CRS. Captain Watson. D. Coy. Loomis. 2 Heavy Bergt Inner of me Heavy Section.	(7)
	8.6.17		Captain Jarvis officer left for leave.	(8)
	9.6.17		Captain Laurel Ramc Tc joined unit.	(9)
	10.6.17		Nothing to Report.	(10)
"	11.6.17		Proceed to EPEHY and Divn station with Captain Nelson Divn O. within this position.	
EPEHY	12.6.17		Tents aid tent in position Tofs. Captain Nelson Rylr Dist. The lines proceed to EPEHY as advanced Hars. Ranede from BUIRE to EPEHY with back in advanced Dressing Station. J.L.H. amb was on 12. P.S.N. D. 14 Rounds. Left J.L.H. Oryson at VILLERS FAUCON under Staff Captain. Hood and advanced Russian Station at EPEHY. Visit by AD.M.S. 2 Leicester tos. Relies in EPEHY, H.S. Latia Posten down to VILLERS FAUCON by R&C Ltd. O.C. of P. H. ABBEY brought up. Come Camp for his Reserve. Rests Back in EPEHY, nearly complete.	(A)
"	13.6.17		Relieve I.R.M.C.O. 5 Days C.C. Reg. aid Post at Willows, New Capt GRANT M.O. 12th R. Irys. as Regt aid Post at Funity Regt: aid Post at Willows, New Capt GRANT M.O. in care of Canadian Dressing Station.	
		10 A.M.	Station fire. Rent Motor ambulance N.A.C. E EPEHY, to Cary in Care of Canadian Nursery weekes abs.	
			Was yellow off of Motor collar radiator tone. B.C.T. Clar sent in D M.D.S.	
		11 am	Casualty bullet wound neck from Bridge Creylem.	

WAR DIARY or INTELLIGENCE SUMMARY

Army Form C. 2118.

8TH CAVALRY FIELD AMBULANCE

Instructions regarding War Diaries and Intelligence Summaries are contained in F.S. Regs., Part II. and the Staff Manual respectively. Title pages will be prepared in manuscript.

(Erase heading not required.)

Place	Date	Hour	Summary of Events and Information	Remarks and references to Appendices
EPEHY.	14.6.17	9 a.m.	2 slight cases transferred from R.H.A. Battery. Two slight wounds 1st Royal Dgns. Visited Jonction Isolé aid post & informed Capt. Wood S/Ama. R.O/c. of 10th Hussars. Two coml. wounded 10th R. Dgns, one slight 10th Hussars put in hands of Town Mayor.	@
"	15.6.17		Very quiet day. Bathe had defectively been put in charge of R.H.	@
"	16.6.17	10 a.m.	1 case of bullet wound 3rd L. Dgts to R.H. Visited Capts. Hood & Doyle. Another very quiet day. No casualties reported.	@
"	17.6.17		Some shelling round EPEHY. 2nd most this morning. Officer K.R.H. slt wound Regtl. Q.	@
"			case H.S.Y. Shell Shock.	@
"	18.6.17		L/Cpl LOWTHER K.R.H. reports from Goat Gallery Hope Shell Shock wound; assist A.D.S. 6:30 p.m. still necessary note despatches to M.D.S. to other casualties.	@
"	19.6.17		Another very quiet day. No casualties. Visited Dr. Scott.	@
"	20.6.17		Quiet day reported. 2 slight wound F.R. Hussars, from Klein-in-Dagout.	@
"	21.6.17		Quiet cloudy day. Lieut. Cpt. Germans & Risopties said a BIRDCAGE. Major Hellin Cavalrie Leger came in at 4 a.m. on enemy despatch armed for war. 15 cases in 9 a.m. to	@
"	22.6.17		A Shell Shock case. me RADC. 1 German airman Pilot knocked down from 15 g. into prisoners by L.O. in A.D.S. Captains 1880. C.F. 15 years out about fees offs to B.O.I.R.E.	@
BOIRE	23/6/17		Relieved by 6 CFA at 5 p.m. returned to camp at BOIRE in marchings.	@
"	24.6.17		Remount to mento to R.Q. cases. Lately arrived mirror any separation. Captain Nelson left to go to study at Ber B.B. Captain Crocket return from leave.	
"	25.6.17		Testing W. report	@
"	26.6.17		Inspected Transport; Civil cases not so difficult to find any Infants colors had still reel keep as place on Imp. Eng. men Leave ordered to Seiscant elegal situation still men I keep in Early Joachin units P.R. Ambulance suffers necessary until term issued will. Tropos - Hoar from A. T. Saten.	@

Army Form C. 2118.

WAR DIARY
or
INTELLIGENCE SUMMARY.
(Erase heading not required.)

Instructions regarding War Diaries and Intelligence Summaries are contained in F. S. Regs., Part II. and the Staff Manual respectively. Title pages will be prepared in manuscript.

Place	Date	Hour	Summary of Events and Information	Remarks and references to Appendices
BUNF.	27.6.17.		Captains Park & O. Edye Kennedy left on leave. Captain Forrest struck off rations on his Leave.	
"	28.6.17.		Received orders preliminary orders of moving. A.D.S. informed that they have 3 C.R.D. Stretchers on loan in their Charge.	(a)(b)(c)
"	29.6.17.		20.0 P's of the S.A.T. inoculator. Tis complete up to date. Heavy section reported went from C of S Rest Station. Captain Davis Kennedy reserves and Lt.	
"	Sunday			
"	30.6.17.		Medical inspection of Heavy section.	

J.G.Plt.
Capt. R.A.M.C.
OC 8th Cav. Fld. Amb.

8TH
CAVALRY
FIELD AMBULANCE.
No............
Date............

Vol 31

140/2298

WAR DIARY
of
8th C. F. Ambulance
for month of
JULY 1917

COMMITTEE FOR THE
MEDICAL HISTORY OF THE WAR
Date 10 SEP. 1917

July 1917

Army Form C. 2118.

8TH CAVALRY FIELD AMBULANCE.

No. ....
Date ....

WAR DIARY
or
INTELLIGENCE SUMMARY.
(Erase heading not required.)

Instructions regarding War Diaries and Intelligence Summaries are contained in F. S. Regs., Part II. and the Staff Manual respectively. Title pages will be prepared in manuscript.

Place	Date	Hour	Summary of Events and Information	Remarks and references to Appendices
BOIRE.	1/7/17.		Nothing to report.	(P)
SUZANNE	2/7/17.		March to Suzanne about 15 kilos.; Many mosquitos into the camp.	(P)
TREUX.	3/7/17.		March continued to TREUX. about 15 Kilos. Very hot & bad hills. Good billets.	(P)
			Horse (P.O) Same march to T.N.S., same Met.	(P)
FRESCHENLIERS	4/7/17.		March continued to FRESCHENLIERS, about 25 Kilos. White good.	(P)
REBREUVIETTE	5/7/17.		March continued to REBREUVIETTE about 15 kilo. Billets good.	(P)
ANTIGNEUL CHATEAU	6/7/17.		March continued to ANTIGNEUL CHATEAU about 20 Kilos. Early Start. Billets good.	(P)
"	7/7/17.		1 Cpl. Hore (Same) left at REBREUVIETTE with tonsilitis ? Sewals taken into 12.CCS.	(P)
			3 men J Rect Guard admitted tonsilitis etc. Iwalds Taken to 12 CCS.	
"	8/7/17.		Lieutenant Dunnaud to England on leave. Not there was no accommodation for In. Patients. All came to right	(P)
			Phat Man to 8 Pts. 5 hz. 3/7 C.C.S. Brant Pashen to 8. CFO at AUCHEL.	
"	9/7/17.		Stores Arc and no. 77 3/3 CCS. Brant Pashen to 8. CFO at AUCHEL.	(P)
"	10/7/17.		Colonel Rhein interim Lt Col C.F.A. from Divn H.Q.	(P)
"	11/7/17.		Re-newed to party expound. Conference at A.D.M.S. no definite instructions re proposals made	(P)
"			Nothing to report.	(P)
"	12.7.17		Held Sport meeting, most successful concert in evening.	(P)
"	13.7.17		Paraded Reed. mounts to Section. Alterations etc. made to tents & lorries W. carrying stretchers	(P)
			No provision hot to guard, tents or grounsheets to current Teo officers charged except some delays.	
"	14.7.17		Officers in PM. & N. be used.	(P)
"	15.7.17		Men are to veterinary Salme in ad usual assignment in event interm & repeat at depot of contract.	(P)
"	16.7.17		Captain Rutleff Romero left send at depot of contract.	(P)
			Nother to Report.	
			Harold to Rev. Bryske Willing area at THIENNES about 25 kilos marches off 3.30 a.m.	(P)
THIENNES	17.7.17.		Route pl. PERFAY about 2.30 kms R 1st HILAIRE & AIRE. Good billets.	(P)

A5834 Wt.W4973/M687 750,000 8/16 D.D. & L. Ltd. Form/C.2118/13.

Army Form C. 2118.

WAR DIARY
or
INTELLIGENCE SUMMARY.
(Erase heading not required.)

8TH CAVALRY FIELD AMBULANCE.
No. ....
Date ....

Place	Date	Hour	Summary of Events and Information	Remarks and references to Appendices
THIENNES.	18/7/17.		Received medical arrangement from A.D.M.S. Proceeded to Motorcar to AIRE & arranged for 4 dental cases a day at to dental centre.	(1)
	19/7/17.		Proceeded to Brigade & Staff Captain re above medical arrangement. Interviewed O.C. 2nd L of C. M.O. Essex Horsery & Consulted Him re above medical scheme, & arrangements made re above & put forward scheme & instructions re above & arrange to operate the scheme at THIENNES & intervening stage to send 4 cases of diphtheria infects and the Infectious Hospital, Officer of Sanitar refunds here, met Captain Davis re Theatre (S.R.A. to 90 & to 39 Dist. Inf.Bde) where the Captain Davis is Medical officer.	(2)
	20/7/17.		Arrangements for keeping 12 patients (sick) in at.	(3)
	21/7/17.		Nothing to report.	(4)
	22/7/17.		Captain Marshall Hoyne returned from 39th Rest Hospital Inches vice Captain Davis Robert at 39 Division Rest Station.	(5)
	23/7/17.		Received Lieut Safford L.D. Molloy H.D.	(6)
	24/7/17.		Nothing to report.	(6)
	25/7/17.			(6)
	26/7/17.		Obtained small hospital or Office where office was & office work was handled in. Received annexed medical arrangement from A.D.M.S. but there & all O.C. units Paraded R.A.P.s & arrangements method of holding Brigade officers O.C. F.A.S. Conference with F.M.O.s & O.C F.H.S no Brush R. Imperture Gogel forward.	(7)
	27/7/17.			(6)
	28/7/17.		Nothing to report.	(6)
	29/7/17.		A.D.M.S. Car Corps inspects to P.M. lection.	(8)
	30/7/17.		War Gas attacked by Germans & Gas lean distribution at paragon from in feat areas, Cases sent Coopalate in Norwalk. 1 Sergt & 10 Wheelwrights sent to 39 Dist. In the Connection.	(9)
	31/7/17.		Raining	(10)

G.O. Offl
Capt. H.S. RAMC.
O.C. 8o Cav. Fld. Amb.

WAR DIARY
of
No 8 Can. Field Ambulance
for the month of
September 1917

Army Form C. 2118.

WAR DIARY
or
INTELLIGENCE SUMMARY.
(Erase heading not required.)

Instructions regarding War Diaries and Intelligence Summaries are contained in F.S. Regs., Part II. and the Staff Manual respectively. Title pages will be prepared in manuscript.

8TH CAVALRY FIELD AMBULANCE

Left 1.

Place	Date	Hour	Summary of Events and Information	Remarks and references to Appendices
AIRE EN ARTOIS	1.9.17		Cav. Corps Horse Show.	
"	2.9.17		Air raid at night.	
"	3.9.17		Air raid reported.	
"	4.9.17		Pte Fleetwood 7/8 Cav. Cafs to Surg: main duties.	
"	5.9.17		Insp by A.D.M.S. Satisfactory except three men with scabies. More showers received in form of dust-rakes, picks & white-wash, soap, etc.	
"	7.9.17		Interdivisional Transport inspection by O.C. A.S.C. Others remain note:- (1) Lt. Horne ambulance several repairs receiving. (2) Horse harness not clean. (3) Spare tools not in G.S. waggon. (now attended to).	
"	8.9.17		Inspection of Ambulance by A.D.M.S. Satisfactory report. Transport & horse lines inspected etc. Catchment to G.T.S. I.O.H. instant. School being restored this is. No hospital with beds. Hospital to be found in next village. Empty cottage found in next village.	
"	9.9.17		Room, front broken, for new hospital. Totally safe and without Capable of holding about 16-20 cases.	
"	10.9.17		More kits. Enquiry Anybody on Britt Hq: Self & Sergt Castle complete inspection of O.A.H.G.S. by A.D.M.S. Kitchen not to good. Gas lecture by I.G.O. Commencing not getting home in Freynville ready for hospital — Pigmy School (O).	
"	11.9.17		Lefs Broadhead + Pte Turner reporting from 1st H.P.S.	

Army Form C. 2118.

WAR DIARY
or
INTELLIGENCE SUMMARY

(Erase heading not required.)

Instructions regarding War Diaries and Intelligence Summaries are contained in F.S. Regs., Part II. and the Staff Manual respectively. Title pages will be prepared in manuscript.

8TH CAVALRY FIELD AMBULANCE

Place	Date	Hour	Summary of Events and Information	Remarks and references to Appendices
H.Q.A.F.A. A.R.F.C.S.	12/9/17.		Exam. 4 nursing orderlies. Rubig School.	(P)
	13.9.17		Letter to Asst. Director of Medical Services of Indian Cavalry Corps re: Chief Master of the Committee, Capt. Lewis medical letter re report of Lieut. Greenhurst.	(P)
	14/9/17		Inspector of horses by Brigadier, horses taken remarkably well: report v. good except that in 2nd & 3rd Cases grooming was bad. Indian Report.	(P)
	15.9.17		Rubig School, pumping.	(P)
	16.9.17		"	(P)
	17.9.17		Fatigue Party (10) to HERVILLE for ambulance Corps. Examined 3 nursing orderlies.	(P)
	18.9.17		Pte. Schley & Cas. Cpls. H.S. Pte. Greenwood. Fatigue party of 5 to YEMANT continued & remained attached with 31st Division ambulance train. Pte. Turner, Reed, Barkerlaw & Pierce transfered to Dental Treatment.	(P)
	19.9.17		H.&M.S. very simple. One horse said to be suffering. Visit by Colonel Rogers RAGEY & A.D.M.S.	(P)
	20.9.17.		Seen Lt Colonel, writes to report.	(P)
	21.9.17		Lecture to report. Captain Marshall returned from duty with No 9. C.F.A. Anti-gas lecture & new equipment.	(P)
	22.9.17		The food by D.D.M.S. Col. Cope's followup points noted. Talk & new equipment. Sgt. Turpin self v. keys Bartle complete. The more Indian Hospital at HANGEVILLE.	(P)
	23.9.17		Hospital cases inspected at HANGEVILLE by Royal Fusiliers by Lt Colonel Hersigham. Everything very satisfactory. Examination of Sergt Palmer.	(P)
	24.9.17		Hospital cases sick to report.	(P)
	25.9.17		Capt. Carey left on 10 days leave to England.	(P)

Army Form C. 2118.

Sept 17. 3

WAR DIARY
or
INTELLIGENCE SUMMARY.
(Erase heading not required.)

8TH
CAVALRY
FIELD AMBULANCE.
No.............
Date............

Place	Date	Hour	Summary of Events and Information	Remarks and references to Appendices
HAMMEN	26.9.17		Nothing to report.	
ARTONS	27.9.17		"	
"	28.9.17		Tactical exercise of 1st C.B. v. 9th C.B. R.M.S. attached but no scheme had been made out for him to take part in. only one R.M.O. was present. This sort of field day is useless as far as the tactical lessons are concerned. R.M.S. of all R.H.A. & T.F. Divs. should come. A.S.C. & rest of lorries, lets also stat of all R.H.A. & T.F. Divs. went hard & explain the object of exps. Exercises & lorries not noted. Not written for.	(B) (B) (B) (B)
	29.9.17		Brigade interviewed me about the P.M.S. at yesterday's tactical exercise. He was not pleased with answers of O.C. P.H. & this question. I pointed out that no chance was given to the P.H.S. as no arrangements had been made to have a further & more practical day has been promised.	(B)
	30.9.17		Nothing to report.	

E.O. Pell
A/M Smith
O.C. 8 CFA

WAR DIARY
of
No 8 Cavalry Field Ambulance
for month of
August 1917

WAR DIARY or INTELLIGENCE SUMMARY

Army Form C. 2118

8TH CAVALRY FIELD AMBULANCE

Place	Date	Hour	Summary of Events and Information	Remarks and references to Appendices
THIENNES	1.8.17		Raining hard. Nothing to report.	
"	2.8.17		Rain continues. Civis getting into very bad state.	(B)
"	3.8.17		First case of diphtheria amongst civilian population. Re-sugar the & passes reports since the arrival of the Brigade at THIENNES. All possible precaution taken.	(B)
"	4.8.17		Rain continues. Recpt of D.M.S. Cav. Corps G baggage cart overhead & inspection. Coys & case forwarded.	(B)
"	5.8.17		Visit of Brigadier.	(B)
"			Conference at H.D.M.S. 3rd Cav. Divn reference the putting aside of L.G.S. wagon on return of Brigade, 8 big return of Brigade Motor Charge for rations, & the attached of M.2 subaltern, & 8 big return sent to receive for rations. Men came to grey, but received L.G.S. wagons of artificer for studs, but R.E. will be and some to 35-lb. at cond. point 4 artificer for studs but carry 30 roll. 2 officer, 1 O. Carry 30 rod. 10 lines 1. R. Heavy section of home stretchers & men subsisting for M.F.T. carried by G. Baxters ambulance & light section & men subsisting for M.A. cart and medical Rept for.	(B)
"			Captain Marshall home, light Pallot, of 3 O.R.S. left and proceed to battalion.	(A)
"	6.8.17		OUDEZON to be duty with the moment. Battalion.	
"	7.8.17		Left for 10 days leave. To England. Handed over Command to Capt. Lund. Adm. T.C.	
"	8.8.17		1st Rev. Command. I went for Capt. S.S. Clark during his absence on leave. Fine. Day.	
"			Visit of DDMS Cav. Corps. Both officer & D.M.S. attend in village. Later, in accordance with RSMS institution, I visited all billets in the village & inspected condition of cooking rooms. Dry & fine.	
"			Day that again in following equipment as now of deficient. Light medical inspection of mud. Found still to be taken by mud & cleaning equipment who often the rain.	
"	9.8.17		Day that again in following equipment as now of deficient. Light medical inspection of mud. Well relieved by travelling the of mud. Battle left clear & ground excellent.	
HAM- EN-ARTOIS	10.8.17		Moved to new billets at HAM-EN-ARTOIS at 11 AM from THIENNES. Billets left clean & ground excellent. Much to provide. Capt NELSON departed on leave for 14 days (inclusive). Men vacated (tents in-to -) left tents. Visit QAOMS. Capt Slaven takes on charge of 8th MSP & S Battery R.H.A.	(A)

Army Form C. 2118.

WAR DIARY
or
INTELLIGENCE SUMMARY.
(Erase heading not required.)

Instructions regarding War Diaries and Intelligence Summaries are contained in F. S. Regs., Part II. and the Staff Manual respectively. Title pages will be prepared in manuscript.

8TH CAVALRY FIELD AMBULANCE

Place	Date	Hour	Summary of Events and Information	Remarks and references to Appendices
HAM-EN-ARTOIS	11.8.17		Day spent in settling into new billets. Visit of ADMS	
	12.8.17		Routine work only. Medical stores and drawn from Lillers. Evacuation this date place to No 19 Stationery Hosp.	
	13.8.17		(7A hospital broken). Accommodation for 20 patients (including 7 sisters) now being in HAM.	
	14.8.17		Routine work. Ambulance wagons being repainted.	
	15.8.17		Received report of 2 civilian casualties of Aeroplane from Sam Officer. Found that they had free beds to AERGUETTE	
	16.8.17		Routine work only. Rather poor weather. Force limb very soft. Men moved from personal to horse lines	
			Rode over area for horse lines.	
	17.8.17		Inspection of "Park" unit by G.O.C. 6th Cavalry Brigade outside village of HAM in absence of month. Park	
			mounted drilled etc. paraded separately.	
	18.8.17		Three OR's sent up to 1st line pack under Capt Marshall with dismounted battalion on account of breakout	
			of 9 Battalion with sickness. No nurse ambulance (Sunbeam D.1 1208) sent to remain with party	
	19.8.17		Handed over command of unit to Capt E.B. Colin in his absence from leave	
	20.8.17		Took over command of unit on return from leave. Airplane raid 2 bombs dropped (cordite)	
			Brigade inspection in marching order & on the march by Capt Boumache. Satisfactory	
			Another air raid - no damage.	
	21.8.17		Very wet.	
	22.8.17		Weekly kit report	
	23.8.17		Captain Lumb. Left & Yorks on temp. medical charge of R.H. Guards during absence of	
			Capt Carrie on leave.	
	24.8.17		Maj. Currie in Division of Eye Hospital Oct 6/8 D.D.H.S. Cav Ofs.	
			Evacuation made in Divisional Horse Show. A Turner awarded 10 Ops. 7 P. M.O.s	
	25.8.17		Divisional Horse Show. Capt. Marshall returns from Leave chief and W. Yorkshire.	
	26.8.17		Captain Tebbitt returns from leave. Engineer N. Hospital Oct 6/8. Captain Harvey.	
	27.8.17		Captain Tebbit took over medical charge of A.G.S. & G. Battery of H.A. Captain Hevins	
			assumes charge of hospital	

Army Form C. 2118.

WAR DIARY
or
INTELLIGENCE SUMMARY.
(Erase heading not required.)

Instructions regarding War Diaries and Intelligence Summaries are contained in F. S. Regs., Part II. and the Staff Manual respectively. Title pages will be prepared in manuscript.

8th CAVALRY FIELD AMBULANCE

Place	Date	Hour	Summary of Events and Information	Remarks and references to Appendices
HAMEN- ARTOIS	28/8/17		Capt. Snowball left for dinner in England. T. Allen war. and H appendices.	A
"	29.8.17		Nothing to report. Has Comm O. believe to reserve overlies arenas.	B
"	30 -		Nothing to report.	C
"	31.8.17		Nothing to report.	D

E.J.C. Hall
Capt. RAMC
OC 8th Cav. Fd. Amb.

WAR DIARY
of
8th Cav: Field Ambulance
for month of
OCTOBER 1917

COMMITTEE FOR THE
MEDICAL HISTORY OF THE WAR
Date -8 DEC. 1917

Army Form C. 2118.

WAR DIARY
or
INTELLIGENCE SUMMARY.
(Erase heading not required.)

Instructions regarding War Diaries and Intelligence Summaries are contained in F. S. Regs., Part II. and the Staff Manual respectively. Title pages will be prepared in manuscript.

8th CAVALRY FIELD AMBULANCE.

Oct 17.

Place	Date	Hour	Summary of Events and Information	Remarks and references to Appendices
HAM-EN-ARTOIS	1.10.17.		Capt. Lewis left for Camp; Maj. at Cav; Capt. Abyad; Capt. Marshall took over later. 2nd in command.	(B)
			Hypnic taken out of R.M.S. Collection & Casualties as a map reference point good.	(B)
			Managers proceed in hospital. To appreciate more potentials.	(B)
	2.10.17.		Nothing of import.	
	3.10.17.		Capts. Lewis & Marshall left for Pas Bruise at Cav. Cops. accident to Brigadier; no serious injury. Notes.	(B)
	4.10.17.		S.59 Div Cav. Cops. inspected R.M.Robin. Did ground & horses. Remarks:	
			(1) Too much athletic, horses carried it no doubtful where I will be of any use with R.M.S.	
			(2) Fwd Scouts too heavily carried	
			(3) Fwd Enemy? malis carried	
			Before post mule and Rectals	
			(4) Hillside Covers for harness. There were outpost wounded sichin for post in Brigade Tactical exercise. I send Nurse out	
	5.10.17.		to Informant. I got out of Conen; and if R.M.O. I were there practice in maps	(B)
			attack on Yves Bois yesterday very successful & possibilities so leading.	
			there for us in the near future because nothing.	
	6.10.17.		Lt.Col. Chisam Marshall & Sarcot Hedon from Gas Bruise	(B)
	7.10.17.		Orders for the Brigade. F more with now area tomorrow. Return Rest post & hospital marquee, evacuated 12 patients to hospital.	(B)
			9 O.R. scouts, arrived & Paid duty to carry by Rita falling trestles & water. Mr. Gaithly got home to put me go into action.	
			It transport left for permanent up with others to Tom move Casernes, lined at 4.30 p.m. for Hypnic Crops at WHITENESS (our Bn. Caps)	(B)

Army Form C. 2118.

WAR DIARY
or
INTELLIGENCE SUMMARY.

(Erase heading not required.)

Instructions regarding War Diaries and Intelligence Summaries are contained in F. S. Regs., Part II. and the Staff Manual respectively. Title pages will be prepared in manuscript.

Place	Date	Hour	Summary of Events and Information	Remarks and references to Appendices
HAM. EN. ARTOIS.	8/10/17		Another Scarus & Rare definitely broken. Orders to move to front notice. Rolled up.	(R)
	9/10/17		Orders to move to front notice cancelled.	(R)
	10/10/17		2nd Field Parade. Hospital reopened.	(R)
			Who B more of our W.Rlts. were temans. Hospital closed. Rolled up.	(R)
	11.10.17		Capt Haney has not yet returned from leave. Unit moved to AIRE D'AILLENNES, PT TENNANT. about 10 kilos. First rate billets left.	(R)
AIRE D'AILLENNES, ST TENNANT	12.10.17		In new area in open order to open hospital for retained cases. Capt. Haney returns to unit from leave until 13th.	(R)
"	13.10.17		Reconne of good billets for men + N.C.O's + Officers first days. 20 horse picket accomodation in new billets. Relation hospital good. Sectn + Reform trained post partners in Syref. Father &c. + two given more accomodation in cottage hamlet.	(M)
"	14.10.17		In dining Hall. Over ten to more horse spaces in cottages hamlet.	(R)
"	15.10.17		Nothing to report.	(P)
"	16.10.17		Orders that Brigade moves into a new area tomorrow.	(P)
BOURS	17.10.17		Brigade moved to new area today. This unit billeted BOURS march of 17-20 kilos; early start 6 a.m. Billets arrangement very bad; billeting party only arrived one hour before arrival of unit. Billets poor, all horses under cover.	(R)
"	18.10.17		An early move to a new area is short of the place.	(R)
"	19.10.17		Some misunderstandg re smoke clothing; clothing brigade party to ascertain details.	(R)
"	20.10.17		What is necessary. Nothing to report.	(R)

WAR DIARY or INTELLIGENCE SUMMARY

Army Form C. 2118.

Place	Date	Hour	Summary of Events and Information	Remarks and references to Appendices
HOUVIN Houvigneul	21/10/17		Marched to HOUVIN. Distance about 17 kils. Got billets etc. Weather showery. Captain Slaney left for temp. duty with D.R. Horses being absence of Capts.	(A)
VIGNACOURT	22/10/17		Switched on a month's leave to England. Marched to VIGNACOURT about 30 kils. A long trying march with many halts. Transport came along well; not strict. dense rain. VIGNACOURT Sr. Nurses well. Lieuts. Home & Eliot's horse got run over at Cookhouse. Horses all under cover.	(B)
"	23/10/17		Major Ceves, R.O. Bones sick. Captain Lennel & I took his morning parade. Hospital, Dispensary & receiving room & office in chateau, accommodation for 12 - patients on the way. In morning Maj. Ceves, Little & his Colonel safe on a trip of visit & got they are good etc. Visited VIGNACOURT R.O. Blum met Capt Lennel, he suddenly had other little & is permanent, also tries to visit him to go to LE TOUQUET. Visits A.D.M.S. see if this is permits, as this is becoming got a ruling as to evacuation of Sick Officers to LE TOUQUET generally so that sick them not lightly so. Hudson etc a nuisance in the Brigade. 1 sick officer where sent only lightly. Have a right to go to Le Touquet with Div Summaries battalion in connection with orders for 20 O.R. to join up with D.G.V.O. in PERONNE area. I have been told while I take its place towards making attacks etc. in PERONNE area every I have been told, two new billets has the character.	(C) (D) (E)
"	24/10/17		Not very good.	(F)
"	25/10/17		Accompanied Hospital Corps, etc. visit to No.2 Stationary at D.H.S. Dental Hospital; Divisions of Croix Rouge stations John B.R.C. and divisions of	(G)
"	26/10/17		Party of 9.20. O.R. left for PERONNE area. Visits FIESELLES. Have baths, fine repairs.	
"	27/10/17		Taken on issue by Sanitary Officer. Office moved from hospital, Reception room re-allotted. Notice of this issued by Brigade H.Q. opened.	

Army Form C. 2118.

WAR DIARY
or
INTELLIGENCE SUMMARY.

(Erase heading not required.)

Place	Date	Hour	Summary of Events and Information	Remarks and references to Appendices
NIEUPORT	29.10.17		Captain Forest to Blew via Regn Coric & hospital at La Panne.	
	30.10.17		Battery to Nieuport. Boxing.	
	31.10.17		M.D.A.S. units visit. Football v Blew. Won.	

E.G. Mell
Capt. O.C. C. C. F. B.

No. 8. Cav. F.A.

COMMITTEE FOR THE
MEDICAL HISTORY OF THE WAR
Date 17 JAN. 1918

Army Form C. 21

WAR DIARY
or
INTELLIGENCE SUMMARY.
(Erase heading not required.)

6TH CAVALRY FIELD AMBULANCE

Place	Date	Hour	Summary of Events and Information	Remarks and references to Appendices
HAVRINCOURT	1.11.17		Captain Forest returned from 3 hrs leave — Regtl Corps havg returned from Lt Toupet.	(a)
"	2.11.17		Letters & report.	(b)
"	3.11.17		Pte Sadham to Corps Vet. for duty (temp) 600 rounds amn.	(c)
"	4.11.17		Inspection of horses by P.V.O. Officer; 5 orderlies to be clipped out.	(d)
"	5.11.17		Nothing to report.	(e)
"	6.11.17		A.D.M.S. visited hospital — White. Captain Nelson returned to duty from 3 days Amiens.	(f)
"	7.11.17		Letters & report.	(g)
"	8.11.17		Capt. F. Lund returned from leave.	
"	9.11.17		Nothing to report.	
"	10.11.17		D.M.S. 3rd Army Hosp paid brief visit & went.	(h)
"	11.11.17		Orders that early snow is likely, these recalled from Corps.	(i)
"	12.11.17		Inspected horses, all except 3 in work: { septic leg, 1 rheumatism acute, 1 trick }	(j)
"	13.11.17		Attended Conference at Brigade Headquarters.	
"	14.11.17		Visits of A.D.M.S. discussed in conference questions of P.M.S. exercise & drill of Pack horses demanded.	(k)
"	15.11.17		{ 1 to carry operating table & A/Station bottles, 2 " 2 sacks of dressings, medical, 3 " 2 sacks of comforts & rations, 4 " officers packs & supplies }	

N.O. Leicestershire Yeo: whilst regtl: is away in the brigade the place of J.B. Brigade. Poets & also instructed in general store etc.

Russ Carl Pritchard

WAR DIARY
or
INTELLIGENCE SUMMARY

Army Form C. 2118.

2 C.F.A.

Nov. 1917

Place	Date	Hour	Summary of Events and Information	Remarks and references to Appendices
DIGNICOURT	16.11.17		Travelling alto inspection. Home took this in Reserve. Officers conference at my office.	(a)
"	17.11.17		Received orders G.4.60/62 from Division in which same notifies that I command the 3 C.F.As on the line of march when disentrained.	(b)
"	18.11.17		March to BRAY. War Diary march tables. 2 P.M. arrived midnight. No talk allowed by O.C. Division either to men or official mess & horses under cover. Col. Robb hotels in Bray good all men & horses under cover.	(c)
BRAY	19.11.17		Visits Brigadier & discussed medical arrangements. Interview Brigade major & R.M.S. from Brigade on leaving BRAY. 1 D.S. wagon with 1 day's rations goes All Echelon on leaving BRAY. C.F.As are disentrained & come under orders of Divns on leaving BRAY. Brewstern in this area to GAILLY. Par unit at Sons S. March to Sir: CFAs to meet area discussed. Ready to form 9.30 a.m. late order to stand to from 6.30 a.m. tomorrow.	(d)
"	20.11.17		Supplies muddled. R.M.S. Supplies from Brigade; but no supplies sent for Henry Seton, ordered by L.to C Station reported in action. Ration R.N. days behind with B. Echelon.	(e)
"	21.11.17		Handing R. L. A.C.D. reports to have no moving up. Sent S. to order R. on to the notice now. Saw Captain Price re supplies. Rations out of action & infantry constipating. Stand to M. Cavalry reports.	(f)
"	22.11.17		Evacuation during last 4 days late been too high. Two is mostly due to 10 Hussars. R.M.Os conferring all Field Days: about those injured on them to receive & deploy machines when Horses have passed.	(g)

WAR DIARY
or
INTELLIGENCE SUMMARY

Army Form C. 2118

8TH CAVALRY FIELD AMBULANCE

Unit: 8th C.F.A.

Place	Date	Hour	Summary of Events and Information	Remarks and references to Appendices
POULAIN-VILLE	23.11.17.		Returned back to billets at POULAINVILLE. White pain. Am hopeful care be made here if we stay.	(A)
"	24.11.17.		Visited Brigade Officers. Team of Army astir as regards possible move here or out. News that a move back to BRAY implies some medical kit for Hospital. Polo up again today. Have hockey.	(B)
			Captain Marshall appointed to M.O. Brigade Surgeon of H.V.S. Sent memos to C.O. reference late hours of buglers in sick from units to M. Louis notice.	(B)
"	25.11.17.		Standing to.	
"	26.11.17.		Notice to move. Accommodation for men here is bad. All horses under cover.	(B)
			Smell hospital to accommodate 10 Patients (Sme). D.A.D.M.S. reports 156 C.F.A. has no accommodation for Patients. I have only sufficient	
"	27.11.17.		for 10. & could not take cases from No. 6.	(C)
"	28.11.17.		Captain Lunt states he will not receive sic context unless he gets a secondary point. Applicates put in for same. 13 sick cases of 7 Hussars from Escodie Infirmary - 15 cases sent in, all sent up 3rd Cav. St. P. to bury a dismounted Brigade up the line, 4 Stretcher bearers 1 mule cart & horse & para St. attached to the battalion from the Brigade from	(D)
			two ambulances.	
"	29.11.17.		Captain Harvey attaches permanently to 10th R. Hussars point. Conference at Brigade Headquarters 18 Dismounted Brigade which leaves for the line tomorrow. Captain Harvey M.O. to 10th R. Hussars to M.O. joins Battalion for 1st Relief.	(D)
			Next day: Football match 8CF.AV. R.F.C. The Brigade will probably move from this area shortly. Won by 3 to 1.	

Army Form C. 2118

WAR DIARY
or
INTELLIGENCE SUMMARY.
(Erase heading not required.)

8 C.F.A.

Place	Date	Hour	Summary of Events and Information	Remarks and references to Appendices
POULAIN VILLE.	30/11/17	10.0 a.m.	Visits A.D.M.S. the morning, 7th C.F.A. in taking over A.D.S. 9th M.D.S. in the Querimesnil Brigade. This unit is to take over the Cavalry Corps Rest. Station at JOINGT. 8th C.F.A. is to remain behind & run a Central Hospital for the horses left in the back area. Visits to 9 Hussars, Captain Haney is left with Remnd Party; visits H.Q. Lerouille Lo., & ret him to meet him after the field Op. & R. Lawson during absence of Captain Haney.	
		12.0	On arrival had at billets found followers orders from Division to "all preparis orders are in abeyance. The Division will be ready to move at 1½ hrs. notice mounted or dismounted on arrival of teams." Sent O.P. cyclist to inform A.D.M.S., packed up & evacuated 23 Patients. Mounts taken to 42 Stationary Hospital with note to O.C. 42 Stationary Hospital, rode to my post at Lavery to send him to many scales, infantry here &c. My report at 2.30 p.m. left Parade & Personal Lent in for its inclusion and reference as soon as possible. Very Many ready to move A.L. 2.30.p.m. Orders now from Brigade & A.D.M.S. that move is on G.A.P. scheme. Orders now from 8.M.S. & send 2 H.O.s & send 2 O.R. on 2 motor ambulances to report at time of the movement to battalion. It's stand up. Ambr. for Hansans to battalion. Please 6 a.m. Motor ambulances morning arrived 12.30.	

G.C.Clayt
Capt. O.C. 8 C.F.A

140/2618.

No. 8. Cav. F.A.

COMMITTEE FOR THE
MEDICAL HISTORY OF THE WAR
Date -1 FEB. 1918

Army Form C. 2118.

WAR DIARY
or
INTELLIGENCE SUMMARY.
(Erase heading not required.)

2/C.F.A

Place	Date	Hour	Summary of Events and Information	Remarks and references to Appendices
PICQUIGNY.	1/12/17		Captain Lewis & Capt. Ribon with S.O.R. with medical equipment left at 7.30 am to report to A.D.M.S. (ref. order mentioned yesterday). Motor Ambulance arrived from 7. C.F.A. to do duty with this unit, which is now responsible for 4th & 8th C.E. Brigade. Brigade Major of above arrangement. Maj. Wynn invited Brigade this & informed Bde. Major of above arrangement. Brigade Major informed that notice to move of that notice. Orders from Brigade that all units probably move to a new area tomorrow.	(A)
BELLOY SUR SOMME.	2/12/17		Moved to new area this afternoon (via Picto). Arrived at new billets 4. p.m. Found orders awaiting to send 1 Officer & 14 O.R.s immediately to relieve & M.S. C.F.A. Captains Forest-Dent in charge of party. Sent from H.Line & III Coys R.S. to 6th C.F.A. 7th C.F.A. sent back to 6th C.F.A.	(B)
"	3/12/17		Bells &c. bore accommodation. & hospital excellent in the chateau & outbuildings. First parade to D.D.R.C.Corps, bands dismissed. Captain Lund to S.O.R. returns from BERNES. N.S. of C.F.A. has arrived here, acting Sergt. of Forest. Captain Lund has signed his contract of transfer to R.H. Irish.	(B)
"	4/12/17		1 Motor Ambulance arrived from 6 C.F.A. In temporary Hd. Qrs.	(B)
"	5/12/17		A.D.M.S. visits unit & interviews Capt. Forest re Bon Enon Company.	(B)
"	6/12/17		Sergt. Hore done with training cart as said 1 week ago.	(B)
"	7/12/17			(B)
"	8/12/17		Capt. Marshall left unit & O.R. Von Huff at O.C.S. TINCOURT. Returns to Unit.	(B)
"	9/12/17		Lieut Hore with training dept.	(B)
"	10/12/17			(B)
"	11/12/17		Sergt. S.O.R. Opt. H. C.F.A. A.D.S. at FRANCOURT.	(B)

WAR DIARY or INTELLIGENCE SUMMARY

Army Form C. 2118.

8TH CAVALRY FIELD AMBULANCE
8 C.F.A.

Place	Date	Hour	Summary of Events and Information	Remarks and references to Appendices
FIELD OF SOMME	12.12.17		Nothing of report.	
	13.12.17		Instead to AULLY-Le Haut Clocher & reconnoitre village as suitable place for 1 S.C.F.A. at two hour daily mvs to VIGNACOURT area in billets.	
			Nothing of report.	
	15.12.17		Captain LUMB left the unit for permanent duty with 2nd Cav. Bde. as Sanitary officer.	
	16.12.17		Colonel Fitzgerald arrived on temporary duty.	
	16.12.17		Major Brent, Red Millington, D.P.E. person arrived o/c Tpt with this Brigade & is attached to this unit.	
	17.12.17		Heavy snow.	
	18.12.17		Lieut. Tovell Lawson held up. 1 day's left rates concerned.	
	19.12.17		Roads still impassable. 3rd days left rates concerned. Tomorrow rations drawn by F.P. wagons from	
			AMIENS.	
	20.12.17		First cont. Patton at 69. Army. CAPTAIN TOVELL arrived back from S.C.C.S.	
			Captain Fitzgerald & Patt. Millington left this unit to S.C.F.A. & 7th Brigade respectively. Details	
	21.12.17		Note of D.A.D.M.S. ref. move of 6th Brigade to S.C.F.A. area & 7th to RIBEAUCOURT area & 7th to ABBEVILLE area. in the near future area this	
			I could undertake & days to S.C.F.A. on this condition of that. it moves to VIGNACOURT. 2 weeks of that. I could claim	
			unit remaining here, it would be of little assistance. For when my Second car is out of workshops I could clear	
			the Brigade arrangement and For when my Second car is out of workshops I could clear	
			most of it to 7th Brigade area from here.	
			Int. released. Returned with Brigadier about midnight 8.10.A.R. Hussars. Poy of Correspondence	
			when sent forwarded to O.A.M.S.	
	23.12.17		First Trgtr. 1 Bath & asst arrived in dubs from 2.0. but ?	
	24.12.17		Xmas dinner & concert for men. Snow commenced & men in evening	
	25.12.17		held further notice this unit is reponsible to clearing	Supply Column
				Reserve Park
				2nd Life Guards
	26.12.17		Heavy snow. Col Cherrier, Lieuts. Lee & Dr. 6 Dr. hind cycle	
			visits cycle of power Leo: stuck in dept.	
			Army advance R.M.O. Prime Co at the line. Lieuts. Kenn Lee, 9th H.S. with softly	
			# 77 O. Reserve Park in case of medical emergency. Matter are withmost the unit	
			starts at later ?	

Army Form C. 2118.

WAR DIARY
or
INTELLIGENCE SUMMARY.

(Erase heading not required.)

Army Troops CAVALRY FIELD AMBULANCE No. 8 C.F.A.

Place	Date	Hour	Summary of Events and Information	Remarks and references to Appendices
FAVL ARRAS	27.12.17		1 motor ambulance & 2 cars from 6 C.F.A. to Jut.	
BELLOY	28.12.17		Brigade HQ left for Camb. Car B 2 "O" Left Para unable to reach horse (Filloux)	
	29.12.17		Troot & snow cond. Car B 10 P ft's stuck in Diff.	
JUMMIE	30.12.17		Thawing. Car B 2nd Lift Guards stuck in Diff.	
	31.12.17		Capt. Randall returned from hy. art. C.C.S.	

G.G. Ashby
Capt.
O.C. 8 CFA

COMMITTEE FOR THE
MEDICAL HISTORY OF THE WAR
Date -4 MAR. 1918

Army Form C. 2118.

WAR DIARY
or
INTELLIGENCE SUMMARY.

(Erase heading not required.)

Instructions regarding War Diaries and Intelligence Summaries are contained in F. S. Regs., Part II. and the Staff Manual respectively. Title pages will be prepared in manuscript.

8 CFA

Place	Date	Hour	Summary of Events and Information	Remarks and references to Appendices
BELLOY d/ SOMME	1.1.18		Nothing to report.	
	2.1.18		Whole car. from exercises. 1 can returned to 8 CFA.	
	3.1.18		An OC. CFA to new ground. The rest of Lieut Floyd about letters to answered. 11 Sickness Cases now in hospital, 4 from Beer. to. Today. Cases of menace in Suffront T	
	4.1.18		Before Captain D'Aoust Jr. Ryland Pratt enlisted Listing Dispose	
	5.1.18			
	6.1.18			
	7.1.18		Time Captain Forsyth NO. Secretaries Co. Returned from leave	
	8.1.18		Influence again. Promotion of more men in R.A.M.C. under present condition seems to be unlikely when carried to promote as vacancies occur in their own unit men from the base men cannot be promoted, much have the last here at the same time of I recommend a man to promotion above to remove 3rd Echelon. Record if the other are wrong that it is often away. Note to him from 3rd Echelon.	
	9.1.18		Note to another unit. mmmmmmm Recd Steward sent to this CFA Saw Staff Captain & told him I cannot accommodate 2 persons in this unit. R.P. elected being a Mr Brothan Person should live at the Division Hopes. Say Captain Proved to write to Lay Captain D about matter.	
	10.1.18		Thaw - some commenced 6 p.m	
	11.1.18		Nothing to report.	
	12.1.18		Captain Cloud orders to report for duty with NZ CFA. Rec'd orders to R.M.S.	
	13.1.18		Dismounted Party returns from Reineken Forest. 7 CFA to still staying up.	
	14.1.18		Instructor Dr P.B. men of Car Corps Signal School. Sanitation of same & personnel of same.	
	15.1.18		Sent N.E. of and as Medical details to School. New Scheme renewed.	

WAR DIARY or INTELLIGENCE SUMMARY

Army Form C. 2118.

8th CAVALRY FIELD AMBULANCE

Place	Date	Hour	Summary of Events and Information	Remarks and references to Appendices
BELLOY EN SANTERRE	16.1.18.		Battery Inspected. Inspection of Kite Balloon section.	(R)
	17.1.18.		Hosp'd N.C.O. Sent with Cemetery Funeral, his O.C. visits each group F.P. Post.	(R)
	18.1.18.		At horse inspection found 1 P.D. horse with symptoms of mange confirmed by P.O. All precautions taken.	(R)
	19.1.18.		Horse scheme continued.	
	20.1.18.		Inspection of D.A.D.M.S.	
	21.1.18.		Captain Forest returned from leave.	
	22.1.18.		Near scheme of "A" substitution of A men in C.F.A. by B men. This scramble letter from A.D.M.S. "A" is substitution of A men with no "A" men reinforcements P.A. guns despatched. I can observe with no "A" men nett of reinforcements if no one clear are not available. Then I can attempt 2 one returns "B" reinforcement if no one clear.	(R)
			Men in hospital 2 men in a sick parade each repeated as yet as any from C.C.S. & stationary & General Hospitals but 6 infantry men. Substitutes caught to me in C.C.S. & stationary & General Hospitals but 6 in Field Ambulances. Replies to this effect.	(R)
	23.1.18.		Further Inspection.	
	24.1.18.		Capt Kendall left for leave to England. 1 man + 2 Logan Officer sent to VIGNACOURT & Infra Batten. Forces in Nicholson Horse Battalion.	(R)
	25.1.18.		Others 10 men or 27th Div'n and see received. Horse issue to Divisible Cavalry of F.B.S.	
			12 NCOs to Avionies to Divisional.	
			12 patient evacuated.	
			Captain Mitchell.	
	26.1.18.		Captain Forest over to Supply Column for things. Chief Jersey over Tractors. Packed up, all patients evacuated.	(R)
BILLAU COURT	27.1.18.		Visit from D.D.M.S. Sent men B. Mitchell: D.O. inoculated: No reference re to Long march & bad road. B. Mitchell: D.O. inoculated: No reference re to 2 Patients upon this arrival at Hosts forest. Cattle lie a member of Brigade heading over.	(R)

WAR DIARY
or
INTELLIGENCE SUMMARY
(Erase heading not required.)

Army Form C. 2118.

8TH CAVALRY FIELD AMBULANCE

Instructions regarding War Diaries and Intelligence Summaries are contained in F. S. Regs., Part II. and the Staff Manual respectively. Title pages will be prepared in manuscript.

Place	Date	Hour	Summary of Events and Information	Remarks and references to Appendices
TERTRY	28.1.18		Marched to TERTRY, about 30 kilos. Had Bryce over to tea at MERAUCOURT. Interviewed new C.O. A.D.M.S. on his way to go to TERTRY. Found accommodation so far as officers & horses is concerned poor so the R.F.W. self completed or horsed to M. hrs. to complete the Nissen huts. No medical or F.O. this were supply enjoying visit.	(A)
"	29.1.18		Found that until B.A. Brown Huts in the area is completed it is impossible to have a sister hospital, hints in Big de Staff, found most of accommodation in area used by Canadian C.F.A. had been taken over Brigade Headquarters & M.H.D. Spedon, but that there were 2 Nissen huts & hospital marquees vacant, got permission to take them over as a temporary measure under accommodation for patients & available for prints Lauterdas C.M.A. units went on truck ride with identification etc.	(B)
"	30.1.18		at TREFCON & went over some Red Cross posts at TREFCON & Villeret of 8 C.F.A. TREFCON not being available until Staff Captain 8 C.C.B. came to see me at Villeret of 8 C.F.A. TREFCON and nice more available, Part of MERAUCOURT is insistent, went to COMMINCOURT 9 from Villeret, but none me available, arranged with Staff Captain of 7 C.B. to visit them tomor at that village we were vacated by Canadian C.F.A. Boys went on carnival, went from 9 A.M.S. Relieved ambulance at Regiment. Prisoner	(C)
"	31.1.18		C.F.A. intervals as men at TREFCON cannot be used back. came home from 6 C.F.A. Stand but of get up R. Drake & 2 life Guards & getting much "DOFULLY" yet. There have all returned from BOFULLY yet. Sent to work on the site.	(D)
"	N.N.1.18		Interviewed R.F. officer who visited Drakville etc. 2 Nissen huts happening to R.A. Brigade Capt. McDonald & M.R. M. Russell. Read 9 R.F.A. hospital where Volunteer of D. Brigade 8 C.F.A. moved to TREFCON 96 to CAULAIS, and medical officer of D.C.F.A.	(E)

J.F. Elliott
H. Floud
O.C. P.C.F.A.

COMMITTEE FOR THE
MEDICAL HISTORY OF THE WAR

Date -8 APR.1918

WAR DIARY or INTELLIGENCE SUMMARY

Unit: 3. C. F. A.

Place	Date	Hour	Summary of Events and Information	Remarks and references to Appendices
TERTRY	1.2.18		Returned R.E. plain rifts material available etc. 2nd Nissen hut having floor laid. Methods & O.R. return from 3. C.F.A. Captain G. Wilson returned from 7th Brigade.	
	2.2.18		3. C.F.A. moves to TREFCON & takes over medical charge of 5th & 7th Brigades. Medical arrangements difficult owing to difficulty in getting hospital gear at TERTRY. Have that not completed and still slow move to East of Péronne. Evacuation necessary under the matron hrs.	
	3.2.18		1 Nissen hut for hospital completed & passed to hospital marquees & 1 female tent details. 2 hospital marquees & 1 female tent details.	
	4.2.18		Officers at Brigade Headquarters (1) received & placed new portable cookers & ovens. (2) Arranged & re-routed equipment. (3) 1st regiment C/7th per Lt. Wm.B. went to ever what we had when he arrived. Captain C. Harcourt & Pt. A Bert at 3rd Div school at SAULCOURT. Officers of R.A.M.S. & Army of Flanders in Emergency (P) Kimaury Hutchin & Harold as possible (2) 1 Surgical consult. Relieve & Receive note. R.A.M.S. Resv. with 1st Aid to division .	
	5.2.18		(3) 3rd A.A. & 3rd E. PAR & 1st Lieutenant & 1/R N.C.Os. had more leave. (4) 3. O.Ps 2nd & Y. N.C.OS 3. O.Ps 2nd. Leading cases for Evacuation. H. Service O.C.D. at HERBÉCOURT. 2nd Reversal returns from 3. C.C.S. A.D.M.S. left for leave.	
	6.2.18		Inspection by F.O.C. Brigade, everything very satisfactory. Orders to send 20 O.Rs to say at officers Home after by private, HESBÉCOURT & Casey or shooting party & go on with medical work.	
	7.2.18		Place Units personnel. The unit is already 2 officers & 16 O.Rs short!	

WAR DIARY
or
INTELLIGENCE SUMMARY

Army Form C. 2118.

Place	Date	Hour	Summary of Events and Information	Remarks and references to Appendices
TERTRY	8/2/18		Went on to Hospital Enquiries well, but still no sign of Messrs Ducks. Rode to 7th C.F.A. at POEUILLY & saw with Staff for Med. He arranged for Carrey nailed the false carrier or front axle. He did not agree with the make of staff and did not do it myself. Dudes issued to C.G. & 29 G. P. 8. The condition of POEUILLY so excellent, a good site & plenty of work done on it.	(a)
"	9.2.18		Ride from STANST BEYOND off CROUCHCOURT receiving Reports of Morries duck & also when it came to fire to (?) Divisions. Ride to 7th Morries Duck. Captain Marshall referred me to Arrangements for Gun Channe Coy(?) L.T.D. Captain Tolson Director Reconnaissance of front TERTRY — DOYCOURT. 7 pm. Colonel Glow, Captain Ackworth & Captain Burchell arr. at some of the Coys. Physician 5-8 Army.	(c)
"	10.2.18		The Coys. Cavalier Physician 5-8 Army.	(d)
"	11.2.18		Domitz arr. (?) Garrison case of more than we can hold in present in closed Door. Two Hair (?) given of room for taking clothes off at bath & better than sames.	
"	12.2.18		March. Quiet day at HERBAUCOURT arrangements satisfactory. Rode to MONT ST QUENTIN & made contact at HERBAUCOURT. School School Captain Toma & referred to Sister Battig, & used specs. at 2.1.(?) L. C.C.C. Sect. hospital. British Base open to men t.d. C. F.A. hospital. Captain bobo. Anyway Nurses being erected, this will complete accommodation in Brigade Hospital. Capt. Thomson R.H. arrived on duty with this unit (R.A.M.C.)	(e)
"	13.2.18			

WAR DIARY
or
INTELLIGENCE SUMMARY.
(Erase heading not required.)

Army Form 2118.

Place	Date	Hour	Summary of Events and Information	Remarks and references to Appendices
TERTRY	14.2.18		[illegible] evacuated with [illegible]	
	15.2.18			
	16.2.18		Scabies hospital now complete & ready for use not occupied Hitherto	
	17.2.18		Reconne from HERBECOURT to TERTRY looking keys & air posts only	
	18.2.18		Motor Report	
	19.2.18		Sister Report	
	20.2.18		Conferred with OC AHT & have arranged removal from later [illegible]	
	21/2/18			
	22/2/18			
	23/2/18			
	24/2/18			
	25/2/18			
	26/2/18			

Army Form C. 2118.

WAR DIARY
INTELLIGENCE SUMMARY.
(Erase heading not required.)

Place	Date	Hour	Summary of Events and Information	Remarks and references to Appendices
TERTRY	27/2/18		Went to TINCOURT to see method of constructing two hospital marquees in order to make one large ward.	
	28/2/18		Nothing to record.	

G.W.Mitchell
Captain
O/C No.8 Cavalry Field Amb.

Jack Smith
Lieut. Col. R.A.M.C.
A.D.M.S. 3rd Cav. Div.

No. 6. Aus. F. A.

WAR DIARY
INTELLIGENCE SUMMARY

Army Form C. 2118.

8th CAVALRY FIELD AMBULANCE

Place	Date	Hour	Summary of Events and Information	Remarks and references to Appendices
TEPTPI	1/3/18		8 Cavalry Bde moved to 6 Cavalry Bde area. Signal Troop horse put into stables also officers. Two 3 army huts handed over to 20 MVS and 3rd DCs under instructions from ADMS. Scabies hospital closed at 12 noon and all personnel not known from MERVACOURT at 6 am. small bomb dropped by E.A. 40 yds S.E. of scabies hospital. No damage done.	
"	2/3/18		Attended conference of O.C.s CFAs of 3rd Cavalry Div. called by ADMS. Personnel and equipment of "modified light western" discussed. Horses inspected by BVO. Two contagious diseases admitted.	
"	3/3/18		Hospital marquees modified to form one large ward. Capt. Marshall and 3 ORs proceeded to 8 army RAMC school, IHAM for course with section.	
"	4/3/18		Inspection of personnel of modified light section by O/C. Report on reconnaissance of "Green Lane" in interest of ADMS	
"	5/3/18		Dental duty. Undiagnosed Salts pastry motor ambulances inspected by O.C. MT. Capt McCallum reported for temporary duty from No. 6 CFA. Light section (modified) inspected by O/C. Visit from ADMS to inspect movement of accommodation available for patients	
"	6/3/18		Harness inspection	
"	7/3/18		Inspection of light section (modified) by ADMS.	
"	8/3/18		Hospital inspected by DDMS 119 Corps + DDMS Cavalry Corps. Informed by ADMS 3rd Cavalry Division that B CFA would shortly be disbanded also that 8 and 9 light sections would shortly proceed to a back area with Home Lots Cavalry Brigade.	
	9.3.18.		Bodies taken from Lieut Jones Ambulance in midst of wet estate cornets with Cmt. Sqn. Cavalry, K. 10, 21.43, mayest L. 30, S.13. Found that 8 Lt Mondo Foundry	

WAR DIARY or INTELLIGENCE SUMMARY

Army Form C. 2118.

Place	Date	Hour	Summary of Events and Information	Remarks and references to Appendices
JERTES.	10.3.18		Light recces made of descents Car. group under Capt. Partridge. Remained below and they return patrols out between Gonnes out in force on defensive crest of S.20.b. but moved before a long field of fire. 20 William cranes (these maker) the disposition which may take forever returns, these maker the disposition have been, if we had been allowed to retain gallery as it would otherwise have been. Some of the horses sent from the other two units were in a stiff and feet state.	(A) (B) (C) (D)
GUYENCOURT.	11.3.18		Pushes to our Lyn positions at GUYENCOURT.	(E)
DOMART.	12.3.18		Lgt sectn marches to DOMART. on arrival at DOMART a bivouac of staff of Louise Gonnes branch out the bipeles interior of DOMART as regard town hi area, got usage of the VILLERS. If all shelter tines. Horses out remainder of position of mile the poshes after. Reinf. moved to VILLERS some ALLY. Medical arrangements completed.	(F)
VILLERS BILLY	13.3.18		It was decided if possible to get the whole Regt. united together from horse G.H.Q and up, as it a question would be done to posits with 3rd Divny as this Horses Det. possessing have this Regt. Mounted arm to Nordern up. Were preliminary orders P.O.R. Instruments: Col Stothert, Capt Jordan, 2/Lt J.B. Sander and group.	(G)
"	15.3.18			(H)

WAR DIARY or INTELLIGENCE SUMMARY

Army Form C. 2118.

8th CAVALRY FIELD AMBULANCE ... 3

J.C.F.A.

Place	Date	Hour	Summary of Events and Information	Remarks and references to Appendices
WILLENCOURT ABBEY	16/3/18		Got supplies round of all units. Carry all kits & equipment, horses into Staff Officer Front & supplies all medical arrangements.	(P)
	17.3.18		Horses taken across my Pate of shoeing near. Capt Sturgeon relief as R.O. Remount Capt Finney life of report of return to Sy Cmd. Capt Sturgeon also Capt Kendrick. Three Sergeants and Horses etc. 2nd Lt Capt Kingsell.	(P)
	18.5.18		To O.C. F.A.F. Captain Langton Sergt — J.O. Supplies wanted, as Supply an Horse 2/2 Life Gds Refs area.	(P)
	19.3.18		Extra Fatay. Interview with O.C. 6th A.C.D. Supply Steven, re Disposal of N.A.T. Vehicles. Classified horses into Rules Driver & Cartle in Remount inspection of D.D.R.	(P)
	20.3.18		14 N.C.O.S. arrived at ALLERY. Parade of Horses before D.D.R. { 11 Classifies remounts. 5 ridden Warriors. 3 riders Cart. 14 retained 4 mules ditto received }	(P)
	21.3.18		Orders for Inspection of Horsetta Remounts N.T.S. Reft area.	(P)
	22.3.18		Visit from D.D.M.S. Cavalry Cops. All personnel joining unit, named cheeks. Void Montpneal. 3' Marcetta horses & medicined. Copt Kneel Bruce to CHAULNES sacrifices for surf. (Bear 5th army) 11 Remounts — 5 unknown Quartermaster.	(P)
	23.3.18		Orders votes at 8 p.m. 11 to ready to lend ambulances by Road & Kny G unknown Destination. Pield Eip. & Mobile ambulance with {1. Seen Pack 2. Gary Pack 3. Pield Pack (5/Stockain) 4. Remounts Pack (Small Arm Section) Roads to Bridge Madeville & Nevure forements Path of months Remounts left of Savergain Caroselies at 6.10 am Reded to the 4/2 one	(P)

Army Form C. 2118.

Army Form C. 2118.

WAR DIARY
or
INTELLIGENCE SUMMARY.
(Erase heading not required.)

S.P.F.A.

Instructions regarding War Diaries and Intelligence Summaries are contained in F.S. Regs., Part II. and the Staff Manual respectively. Title pages will be prepared in manuscript.

[Stamp: 9TH CAVALRY FIELD AMBULANCE]

Place	Date	Hour	Summary of Events and Information	Remarks and references to Appendices
MILLERS from AILLY	24.4.18.		Entrained at Longpré, Newcastle B.A.M. following also received {12.9.14 H.F.G.S., march mounts by road to 3 Henry Bry, 3rd Cavy Barracks} by lorry to 3rd Cavy Barracks {7 pm. 4.11.8}	
			No medical arrangements made for the B.S.S. on Ambreuse Depôts to etc. informed me the two Car medical staff of unit suffered heavy & great (R), Newcastle I requested to man by road to Def. 201 or 262 initial. Relieved Captain Stack, F.A.M.C., to him be made remain behind and pay interviews Captain O'Conor, R.A.M.C., I informed him to road to Longpré from Station of 2oth of the total at Longpré a.m. 4.1.F.S. to Bray. 5.15 Innoman for D.S.	(B)
	25.4.18. 26.4.18.		Last no further orders, came back at 11am to par. Arrangements were gone into. After 4 group one, in to man by road or 279 (a) War order continueous again. { 5.15, no further to remain as reinforcements. Stretched until 12 march up to Car are War order continueous again. 2 to move 1 mounted by at 2 tour available}	(D)
	27.4.18.		Medical arrangements made for the move of Cav.S. and 1 instn. attacks to brigade until by com. to Comm. Division today. Captain Reid arrived 6 a.m. wait, & Off to S.C.O. Respective visits Captain Stack & O'Connor returned to Hq.Q. respective units Household Bayonet Left area this respected to march went Bivited oc Left to MENACOURT 6a.m. as information of more was given to Left to MENACOURT Rest night a ride up any time at MEGUNCOURT the office. Last night a mother as closes White. No orders no news. Until Left Bayonet oc. closes White	

Army Form C. 2118.

WAR DIARY
or
INTELLIGENCE SUMMARY.
(Erase heading not required.)

Instructions regarding War Diaries and Intelligence Summaries are contained in F. S. Regs., Part II. and the Staff Manual respectively. Title pages will be prepared in manuscript.

Place	Date	Hour	Summary of Events and Information	Remarks and references to Appendices
VILLERS sous AILLY.	28/3/18.		Two Squadrons since the left moved to 1st C.D. 3 a.m. this morning. 1 Squadron & Hqrs here till the afternoon. Lieut Capt: Etherington R.A.V.C. to join us here vice Captain O'Connor whom 2 Sqns and ret: Capt. O'Connor to attend to sick Capt. E. could join and not ret.	B
"	29.3.18.		No sick. Inspection of remaining Squadron. Rode to, left this morning. 12.0 Sqr long moved & ready to move as a unit. 12.30 L.V.O order for Veterinary Officer of the unit to move. Unit moved from "D" L.V.C. oral for Veterinary Officer & here scarce more in hour 2" V.C. I gave him the necessary information before him leave. rather with fewer munition. Just was Short I horse.	B
—	30.3.18		No sick. I with ambulance returns from chief with Stamford Bridge.	B
—	31.3.18		Followed with 9 B.A.S. Cav Corps. The unit is now to act in Emergencies for Cavalry Capt: Same. Taken are Command of Austlee. C.F.A. & S.A.Co don't contribute, Steno of Sens all Austlee ambulances I aother cycles.	B

J.G.O[Mc] W
P.A.M.E.

140/2700.

21 Cavalry Field amb.

COMMITTEE FOR THE
MEDICAL
6 JUN 1918

Army Form C. 2118.

WAR DIARY
or
INTELLIGENCE SUMMARY.
(Erase heading not required)

Place	Date	Hour	Summary of Events and Information	Remarks and references to Appendices
VILLERS-FAU-BOIS	1.4.18		Nothing to report.	
	2.4.18		Advise that Major Mc Phail over Command	
	4.4.18		Orders to leave Yale over command of No. 2. C.F.A.	
			M.O.S. recruits & leave for 3rd & 2nd Cavalry Division	
			Handed over command of No. 2 C.F.A. to Captain Holt. D.S.O. R.A.M.C.	
	4.4.18		Took over command of No. 8. C.F.A. from Lt. Col. E. E. Colbeck. R.A.M.C.	
	6.4.18		Medical Equipment evacuated to No. 13 Base Depot Medical Stores under orders from D.D.M.S. Cavalry Corps.	
	8.4.18		Elev. horses. L.D. Remounts sent under orders of D.D.R. Cavalry Corps to 3rd Cav. Bde.	
			BELLENCOURT; four of these returned as not wanted.	
			Warning Orders received for despatch of 5 Sergeants, 8 Corporals, & 69 men & A.D.S. Hosp. supplies to France to go to Base for Disposal.	
			14.5.6. 2nd 39 & 58 & D.R's Supplies to France to go to Base for Disposal.	
			[D.H.S. 4 Army No. P.16/187. & A.D.M.S. Cav. Corps No. 10/380]	
	9.4.18		3rd Cav Bde. wants for two more L.D. - Despatches. Ordnance Stores handed in. 16 LONG PACK	
			Orders from D.D.M.S. to complete demobilisation. 4 Aust. Personnel. 13 NCOs	
			& 69 privates to Infantry Divns W.O. remains to Base.	
	10.4.18		Remaining 2 L.D. horses to 3rd Cav. Bde.	
	11.4.18		8 Cav. F.D. Ambs. broken up, & handed over command in toto to D.D.M.S. Cav Corps.	
			Transport to A.H.T.D.	

E. STONE
Capt R.A.M.C.